GLORIOUS DEEDS
OF AUSTRALASIANS IN THE
GREAT WAR

Books of Topical Interest.

The Real Kaiser.
Crown 8vo, cloth. Price 1s. net.
[*Third Edition.*

Sketches in Poland.
By FRANCES DELANEY LITTLE.
12 Illustrations in Colour.
Demy 8vo. Price 9s. net.
[*Second Edition.*

Field Notes from the Russian Front.
By STANLEY WASHBURN.
Demy 8vo, 60 Illustrations. 6s. net.
[*Fourth Thousand.*

At the Front with Three Armies.
By GRANVILLE FORTESCUE.
Demy 8vo, 30 Illustrations. 6s. net.
[*Second Edition.*

Germany and The German Emperor.
By G. H. PERRIS.
Demy 8vo, 520 pp. Price 2s. 6d. net.
[*Fourth Edition.*

War, Religion and Science.
By REV. J. B. HUNT.
Crown 8vo, cloth. Price 2s. net.

Germany's Swelled Head.
By EMIL REICH.
Crown 8vo, cloth. Jacket in Colours. Design by Kapp.
Price 1s. net.
[*Ninth Edition.*

Daphne in the Fatherland.
By ANNE TOPHAM, Author of "Memories of the Kaiser's Court." Price 1s. net.
[*Fourth Edition.*

LONDON: ANDREW MELROSE, LTD.

General Birdwood, in charge of the operations at Anzac

Frontispiece.]

GLORIOUS DEEDS
OF AUSTRALASIANS
IN THE GREAT WAR

By
E. C. BULEY
Author of "Australian Life in Towns and Country."

The Naval & Military Press Ltd

Published by
The Naval & Military Press Ltd
5 Riverside, Brambleside, Bellbrook
Industrial Estate, Uckfield, East Sussex,
TN22 1QQ England

Tel: +44 (0) 1825 749494
Fax: +44 (0) 1825 765701

www.naval-military-press.com
www.military-genealogy.com

In reprinting in facsimile from the original, any imperfections are inevitably reproduced and the quality may fall short of modern type and cartographic standards.

PREFACE

IN the course of writing this book I have interviewed some hundreds of wounded Australasian soldiers in London hospitals. From their narratives, delivered with a modesty which I have not sought to reproduce here, I gathered much material not obtainable in the short official accounts given of their exploits.

The temptation to record individual deeds of remarkable bravery has been strong, but in most cases it has been resisted. This comparatively small force, which has suffered 25,000 casualties in less than five months, consists of men who are all heroes. After the first few days on Gallipoli, its officers recognized the impossibility of officially recognizing deeds of bravery, and practically no awards have been made since the end of April.

I have collected a large number of remarkable instances of gallantry, but I have concluded that to mention these would be invidious, since the bulk of such exploits has not come under my notice. Such an exception as I have made in the case of Private Simpson, the dead hero of the Ambulance section, will be pardoned. No Australasian ever speaks of him without saying, "He earned the V.C. a dozen times."

I have heard Australasian officers recount deeds of wonderful bravery which they have not cared to report, because "Any of my men would have done the same"; and, in my attempt to record the main incidents of this great adventure, I am constrained to accept this very high standard of duty. Its effect has been to win for Australasian soldiers a reputation for "daredevil bravery" in the mass, and to ignore the supreme efforts of the individual.

I have to thank the *Daily Mail* for the permission to reproduce three of the wonderful exclusive photographs its enterprise obtained from the Anzac zone; the *British Australasian* for the use of all the remaining photographs with which the book is illustrated; and the *Weekly Dispatch* for permission to reproduce matter which first appeared in that paper.

Finally, I have spoken to no wounded Australasian in this country who has not taken occasion to mention the great kindness shown by the people of Great Britain. Many of them, hearing that I was writing a book on Australasia's part in the war, have asked me to mention this. Their thankfulness has been so spontaneous, and they have been so profoundly touched, that I have ventured to refer to it. Their gratitude cannot be too widely made known on this side of the world; nor can the attentions which elicited it be too freely indicated to those who sent them from Australasia.

CONTENTS

CHAP.		PAGE
I	THE LONG BLACK SHIPS	11
II	THE END OF THE RAIDER "EMDEN"	27
III	IN THE LAND OF PHARAOH	45
IV	THE BATTLE OF BRIGHTON BEACH	55
V	OCCUPYING THE LAND	71
VI	POPE'S HILL AND GABA TEPE	91
VII	THE CHARGE AT KRITHIA	103
VIII	THE BATTLE OF QUINN'S POST	117
IX	A THORN IN THE FLESH	129
X	FILLING THE GAPS	143
XI	HOW IT STRIKES AN AUSTRALASIAN	159
XII	THE MAN WHO WASN'T LET	171
XIII	SAID AN AUSTRALIAN OFFICER	183
XIV	THE HEART OF EMPIRE STIRRED	197

CONTENTS

CHAP.		PAGE
XV	The Armies of Australasia	213
XVI	Clearing the Pacific	225
XVII	The Youngest Navy in the World	235
XVIII	The Reward of Valour	249
XIX	The Australasian Soldier	265
XX	Lonesome Pine and Russell's Top	277
XXI	The Mighty New Zealanders	289
XXII	The Night March,—and Afterwards	305
XXIII	The Band of Brothers	315
XXIV	A Tribute to the Turk	329

LIST OF ILLUSTRATIONS

	FACING PAGE
Sir George Reid, High Commissioner for the Australian Commonwealth, 1914–15. . *Frontispiece*	
Australian Infantry Training at Broadmeadows	12
Troops Leaving Brisbane	18
The Australians returning to Camp at Mena, in Egypt	46
Australian Soldiers at the Foot of the Pyramids	48
Sir George Reid, High Commissioner for the Commonwealth, Reviewing the Australian Expeditionary Force at Mena Camp, Egypt	50
Transports bearing the Australasians to Anzac Cove	58
The Landing at Anzac Cove on Sunday, April 25, 1915	62
Shrapnel bursting over Anzac Cove	66
Roll-call on Brighton Beach. The Sad Scene after an Engagement	76
General Birdwood, in charge of the Operations at Anzac	82
General James McCay, commanding 2nd Brigade, Australian Infantry	96
The New Zealanders Reviewed at Heliopolis	106
General Bridges, who commanded the 1st Expeditionary Force from Australia	112
General Legge, who succeeded General Bridges	114
General Monash, Commander of the 4th Brigade, Australian Infantry	118

LIST OF ILLUSTRATIONS

	FACING PAGE
Australian Field Artillery in Action	120
Map showing the stretch of Gallipoli Peninsula from Gaba Tepe to Suvla Bay	130
General Sir A. J. Godley commanding the New Zealanders and the 4th Brigade, Australian Infantry	144
A New South Wales Battalion, ready for the Front	150
The Canterbury Section of the New Zealand Expeditionary Force	154
Colonel Sir Newton Moore, in Charge of the Australasian Depôt at Weymouth	184
The Valley of Death	192
The Australian Submarines AE 1 and AE 2, both lost in the First Year of War	228
Rear-Admiral Sir George Patey, commanding the Australian Squadron	230
H.M.A.S. *Australia* in Sydney Harbour	238
The Governor-General of Australia	244
Captain Richardson of the 1st Brigade	252
Farewell to the Troops in Melbourne	266
The Last March through Sydney Streets	272
A Battery of Australian Field Artillery going into Action	280
A Typical Trooper of the Australian Light Horse	284
A Battalion of New Zealand Mounted Rifles	290
Australian Guns in Action before Sari Bair	308

THE LONG BLACK SHIPS

CHAPTER I

THE LONG BLACK SHIPS

ON November 1st, 1914, there steamed out of the harbour of Albany, in Western Australia, three long lines of great ocean steamships. At their head proudly steamed the Australian cruiser *Melbourne*; the procession was brought up in the rear by another Australian cruiser, the *Sydney*. So the long black ships, forty in all, set out from the last port of Australia in the golden Southern spring, bearing the army of Australasia to the Antipodes in the Old World.

If another such army has ever been seen, it must have been a goodly sight. Each man was a volunteer, who sailed away to fight, not so much as a duty—but as a proud privilege. For that privilege many thousands of fine young men had competed unsuccessfully; those selected were truly the very pick of the flower of the youth and strong manhood of Australasia. The ranks contained men from every class of life. A young barrister, who had relinquished a practice worth some thousands a year, had as his fellow ranker a kangaroo shooter from the far remote bush fastness. Well-to-do young farmers rubbed shoulders with architects and miners, shearers chummed up with city clerks. Men of all grades were bound together by the common cause that had impelled them to take up arms.

The Australasian army was a democratic army. The officers held their rank for no other reason than their fitness to command. Social station counted for nothing; soldier-like qualities alone decided the allotment of commissions, and of appointments to the non-commissioned grades. In one regiment the major was a stockbroker's clerk; the stockbroker himself, formerly the chairman of his stock exchange, was glad to serve in the same regiment as a private. Many of the officers, and especially the non-commissioned officers, had seen much active service in the Boer war. In the ranks there was a strong leavening of the young soldiers who were the product of the system of compulsory national service adopted throughout Australasia only a few years before.

Physically, the men were as near perfection as could be attained in so large a body. The average height of the 20,000 Australians was 5 feet 8 inches; the 8,000 New Zealanders averaged quite an inch more. One battalion of Australians averaged 5 feet 10 inches; while New Zealand again outdid this figure with a battalion averaging an inch

Australian Infantry Training at Broadmeadows.

better. The 12,000 horses they took with them were the very pick of two countries renowned for the stamina and quality of their horseflesh. Their equipment was all of Australasian manufacture; the khaki of their uniforms the best that could be made of the best wool the world produces, their rifles, their ammunition, and every last trifle of their outfit all home-made, and all designed to show how well the Southern Nations could answer a sudden call on behalf of the Empire. It was the first instalment of Australasia's vindication of the promise made by the Prime Minister of Australia : " the last man and the last shilling."

The offer by Australasia of this substantial aid in fighting the battles of the Empire was made before the war-cloud had burst upon Europe, but when the prospects looked very threatening.

The actual outbreak of war was anticipated by the Governments of the Commonwealth and the Dominion of New Zealand by offers of every loyal support. " All Australian resources are for the Empire's preservation and security," declared Mr. Cook, then the Australian Prime Minister; a sentiment crystallized by Mr. Andrew Fisher, then leader of the Opposition and now Prime Minister, in the phrase, " Australia will stand by to the last man and the last shilling " ; which has become the war motto of the Commonwealth. The Prime Minister of New Zealand, Mr. Massey, said

New Zealand would send an expeditionary force, and would support the Empire to the utmost of its resources. A stirring scene followed in the New Zealand Parliament, when the members rose spontaneously and sang " God save the King."

The loyal messages of the Australasian Governments were acknowledged by King George in the following cable :—

"I desire to express to my people of the Oversea Dominions with what appreciation and pride I have received the messages from their respective Governments during the last few days. These spontaneous assurances of their fullest support recall to me the generous self-sacrificing help given by them in the past to the Mother Country. I shall be strengthened in the discharge of the great responsibilities which rest upon me by the confident belief that in this time of trial my Empire will stand united, calm, resolute, trusting in God.

"GEORGE R.I."
"LONDON, *August* 4.

This was acknowledged by New Zealand in the following terms :—

"I am desired by the New Zealand Government to acknowledge your Majesty's gracious message, and to say that, come good or ill, she, in company with the other Dominions and Dependencies of the Crown, is prepared to make any sacrifice to maintain her heritage and her birthright

LIVERPOOL, *Governor General.*"

Australia made a specific offer of 20,000 men as a first instalment for an expeditionary force, which was promptly accepted, as was the offer of the Australian navy. New Zealand offered 8,000 men as a first instalment, and these were also accepted promptly. The work of selecting the best men from the many thousands of eager applicants was a difficult one. New Zealand had 30,000 men in camp at the time, training under the system of compulsory national service. They volunteered for service abroad practically to a man. No immature boys were selected, the age limit being twenty ; and in the end it was necessary to ballot for places among the large number of suitable men who applied for places in the Expedition.

In Australia equal enthusiasm was shown. The age limit here was nineteen, which excluded a large number of the youths training under the Australian system of compulsory service. The medical tests were very severe, as were the tests for horsemanship in the cavalry brigades. Australia had to deny thousands of highly suitable men the privilege of serving in the first contingent,

Troops leaving Brisbane.

but 10,000 of these were put into training at once in order to be ready for a second instalment.

An example of the eagerness to enlist was afforded by the case of a young Queensland grazier, who mounted his horse and, as a preliminary, rode 460 miles from his place at Cooper's Creek to the nearest railway station, whence he travelled by train to Adelaide. He wished to join a Light Horse regiment, and finding there was no vacancy in South Australia, he set off to Hobart, in Tasmania, by boat. There he was also unsuccessful, solely because all the vacancies were filled. Not to be denied, he took boat to Sydney, where he found his place at last, after having travelled over 2,000 miles, on horseback, by train, and by steamer, to serve as a private soldier in the Empire's cause.

The instance is not unique; it is rather typical. Men went willingly under the surgeon's knife for the removal of physical excrescences or defects which were held to incapacitate them for service. Those who could not find a place in the Australasian armies took their passages literally by hundreds to Great Britain, there to enlist in the new armies that were being gathered by Lord Kitchener for training. Others obtained promises of places in future contingents, and at once went into camp for practical training in all the duties of a soldier on active service. The men selected for the first contingent threw themselves into the work of preparation with a splendid ardour, that shortened the time of preparation and permitted a speedy dispatch of the troops to the old world. The actual work of embarkation began on October 17, and was concluded on October 22, so that 20,000 men and 9,000 horses were got on the transports in five days, a sharp bit of work. Before the actual departure, General Bridges sent the following message to the people of Australia:—

"I hope to report that the conduct of the Australians, both in camp and on the field, is worthy of the trust imposed upon them by the people of the Commonwealth. The men are a fine lot, soldierly and patriotic. I am grateful to the soldiers and citizens for the help they have given me in organizing and preparing the force now about to do its part for the good of the Empire. I venture to express the hope that no matter how great the demands on their patience, the Australian people will see to it that there is no diminution of their determination to face their responsibility. This spirit cannot fail then to pervade the troops."

Mr. Pearce, the Minister for Defence, sent to the troops on their departure the following message:—

"Upon the force devolves the honour and responsibility of representing Australia and of performing Australia's share in the great Imperial effort in the interests of justice, honour and international integrity. The ultimate issue of that undertaking can never be in doubt, but its attainment demands a steadfast display of the British qualities of resolution and courage, which are yours by right of heredity. The people of Australia look to you to prove in battle that you are capable of upholding the traditions of the British arms. I have no fear that you will worthily represent the Commonwealth's military forces. Your presence among the Imperial forces has, however, a wider significance, as representing the solidarity of the Empire and the Imperial spirit of loyalty to the King."

And now the men of Australasia are embarked on their mighty adventure. Six months later they were to thrill the Empire with a feat of arms as brave and brilliant as anything contained even in the annals of this, the greatest war of all times. So much they hardly dared to hope then, but they strove by every means in their power to keep themselves fit for the ordeal to come, when they would be matched against the trained soldiers of the greatest and proudest military Power history has ever known.

A glance around those forty troopships would reveal an interesting object lesson in the production of new types of the great Anglo-Saxon race. These are all picked men, whose parentage consisted of the same kind of Britons, drawn from the four root stocks of the islands of Great Britain. But the wide range of climate permitted between the tropical plains of North Queensland and the rugged fastnesses of the mountains of the New Zealand Southland has already produced types so divergent that it is hard to believe that they sprang from the same stock.

Compare McKenzie of Townsville, Queensland, with McKenzie of Dunedin, New Zealand, and the difference is apparent. They may be cousins: such things occurred in that wonderful army of Australasia; but the Northerner is dark, slight, lean and wiry. The lines are bitten in his browned face by exposure to many a glaring day in the merciless direct rays of a tropical sun. His broad shoulders and narrow hips make him an ideal athlete, but he is loosely built. He walks with a swing; his movements look slower than they really are; the sun has given him something of a languor that is not all graceful. But the fire of a high courage burns in his dark eyes, and the sea breezes have already brought a touch of colour to the pallor of his cheek. He is in superb physical health, for all that he is so sallow and hard bitten.

McKenzie of Otago weighs two stone more, though he has no whit of advantage in height. He carries no spare flesh, but is a big-boned, thickset fellow, brought up on mutton and oatmeal. His cheeks are rosy and tanned with the salt wind that never ceases to blow over the wholesome island where he grows rich harvests of grain and tends his plentiful flocks. He is a stiff, great fellow, as hard as nails, and as healthy as a big bullock. His keen blue eyes look out from under a smooth brow unfurrowed by any care. He comes from a land where there is no want; his million or more of fellow New Zealanders have not yet built a big city or created a huge fortune. Easy prosperity, an abundance of physical well-being, and a continual strife for high moral excellence are the characteristics of his country, where the death-rate is the lowest in the world and the sale of intoxicants is subject to closer restriction in peace time than anywhere else in the Empire.

Between these two extremes are all sorts of modifications; the Tasmanian, who grows apples on the sunny borders of the beautiful Huon rivers and enjoys a country that resembles in many of its features the rustic beauty of the best parts of Southern England. He is a big, stocky fellow, this Tasmanian, with something of the rustic simplicity of an English yeoman. But he is not by any means as simple as he appears. Now look at Tommy Cornstalk from New South Wales, tall and lanky, slow of speech and swift as a miracle in action. Hear his queer slang as he talks of his "cobbers" or mates; and shrewdly reckons his chances of seeing Australia again within a reasonable number of years. The Victorian from the rich Western plains is a stockier man, who has an intimate acquaintance with that exasperating animal the cow. Butter has been to him a means of realizing prosperity; from his early youth he has milked so many cows every morn and evening. And when he wishes to express his opinion of the Germans he calls them cows. It is his last term of abuse.

The West Australians, for some reason not yet apparent, are, as a class, the heaviest and stoutest of Australians. They number many a jack-of-all-trades in their ranks, for they have learned to turn their hands to many things. They are bronzed by a climate where the sun seldom fails to shine brilliantly; healthy, shrewd, sane and full of reckless courage. The South Australians approximate more nearly to the Cornstalk type, and from them are drawn some of the finest riders in the ranks of Australia's celebrated Light Horse.

The speech of these Australasians varies remarkably. The short-clipped speech of the men from the coastal cities contrasts strangely with the monotonous drawl of the bushmen. In the New Zealanders the old accents survive strangely; many of them talking Scotch as broad as the men of a Highland regiment. Others speak English of a remarkable purity of accent, though strangely tinged with the slang of the shearing shed, the stable and the bush track.

Of the 631 officers and 17,305 men comprised in the Australian contingent, twenty-two officers only and 6,098 men had seen no previous service. The large remainder were veterans of the Boer war. Only 190 officers and 1,451 men were married, the bulk of Australia's soldiers being single men. Eighty-two per cent. of the officers and 73 per cent. of the men were of Australian birth, the ranks containing a fair percentage of "new chums" of comparatively recent arrival from Great Britain.

Their conditions of service were as follows:—

Rates of Pay.—Lieutenant, 21s. per day; sergeant, 10s. 6d. per day; corporal, 10s. per day; private, 6s. per day.

Separation Allowance.—Married members receiving less than 8s. per day—(a) for wife living at home, 1s. 5d. per day; (b) for each child under 16 years of age, 4½d. per day. A similar allowance as in (a) is paid to the mother of a member who is solely dependent upon him for support.

Pensions.—Payable to widow on death of member of the forces or to a member on total incapacity:—Lieutenant, £91 per annum; sergeant, £70 per annum; corporal, £68 per annum; private, £52 per annum. In addition, on the death or total incapacity of a member, for each child under 16 years of age, £13 per annum. In the case of total incapacity, the wife in addition receives half the rate specified above for the respective ranks.

Under these conditions they were heading Northwards, daily approaching nearer to that Old World where the war flame burned so fiercely. For many days nothing occurred to break the regularity of the discipline by which they kept themselves fit for the great task they had undertaken ; then the monotony of their journey was disturbed by an event which startled them into a sudden realization of the grim imminence of battle and death.

THE END OF THE RAIDER "EMDEN"

CHAPTER II

THE END OF THE RAIDER "EMDEN"

AT 6.30 a.m. on the morning of November 9 the *Melbourne* was steaming at the head of the three long lines of transports when she picked up a wireless message from the cable station at Cocos Island. The message was imperfect, but conveyed to the *Melbourne* the fact that an enemy warship was then off the island. The convoy was at the time about sixty miles away from the island, so that it was obvious there was no time to be lost. The *Melbourne* was the flagship, and her commander was responsible for the safety of the transports, he had, therefore, to deny himself the supreme pleasure of setting off to deal with the stranger. He sent instead instructions to the *Sydney*, which at once set off, gathering speed as she went.

The excitement on board the *Sydney* was intense. It was an open secret that the notorious *Emden* was somewhere in that neighbourhood, and every soul on board, from Captain Glossop to the two boys who had been taken aboard at Sydney from the training ship *Tingara* at the last minute, was fervently praying that it might be the sea-raider which had sunk more than twenty British merchant vessels, and bombarded Bombay. Down below the stokers were at work like demons; a significant sentence in Captain Glossop's official report afterwards revealed how well they worked. He reported that the engines worked splendidly, developing a higher rate of speed than upon the official trials of the ship; as a matter of fact, the crew worked her up to the great speed of twenty-seven knots.

Meanwhile it may be as well to explain just what had happened at Cocos Island. At five o'clock on the evening of November 8 the inhabitants, who were all officials connected with the cable and wireless stations there, noticed a strange warship approaching the island. She paid no heed to their wireless signals, but after approaching very close, stood away again at night time. Early in the morning she again appeared, and as nothing could be made of her, and she was lowering a boat, a wireless call for help was sent off at random. The stranger tried to obliterate this by sending strong wireless calls, which accounts for the message reaching the *Melbourne* in a mutilated condition.

The message was despatched just in time, for three boats put to land with a strong party on board. They were Germans, and at once took possession of the station, and began the work of dismantling it without any delay.

The *Sydney* was now making good time, and at a little after nine o'clock sighted the island, seventeen miles away. To the right of the island could be seen the smoke of a steamer, quite stationary; then the people on the *Sydney* knew they were in time. They were going so fast that all that could be seen of them from the island was a great plume of smoke and a mighty bow wave. That was enough for the *Emden*—for the stranger was, of course, the German corsair. "If that is an Australian cruiser," said the captain, von Mueller, "I'm going to sink her." Out he put to make good his vainglorious boasting, and the distance between the two vessels rapidly decreased.

There was an international group of spectators for the wonderful ocean duel that followed. The people of the cable station gathered on the roof of their building to get a view of the fight; and they were joined there by the members of the German landing party, who had no time to rejoin their ship. The manœuvres of the two vessels were dictated by their armaments. The *Emden* had guns of only 4-inch calibre, and it was her policy to fight at comparatively short range. The *Sydney* had eight 6-inch guns, and Captain Glossop was determined that she should enjoy the tactical advantage due to her by reason of her heavier metal.

The *Sydney's* people were all aglow with excitement, but level-headed withal. Many of them were young Australians, members of the newest navy in the world, and determined that in the first important action fought by that navy all concerned should do it credit. Lads of nineteen, with eyes ablaze with excitement, stood as coolly at their guns as the veterans of a dozen sea fights might have done. The two boys from the *Tingara* carried ammunition about the decks at a steady run, laughing and whistling with glee.

The ships were now steaming parallel courses at a distance of about five miles, the *Emden* trying to get closer and the *Sydney* outmanœuvring her. The order was given on the *Sydney* to load, when the *Emden* fired the first shot of the duel, a salvo which went harmlessly over the *Sydney*; as intended, for it was meant to give the German gunners the range. The *Sydney* replied similarly, with a broadside from her port guns; and the fighting had now begun in real earnest. It was about a quarter to ten in the morning, with a calm sea and a clear atmosphere.

The *Emden* began with some very good shooting; its excellence was emphasized by the fact that the German gunners were firing at the extreme range of their guns, and had to use an elevation of about thirty degrees. The shots that struck the *Sydney*—there were ten in all, and all in the first ten minutes of the fighting—were falling at such an angle that their hole of exit on the starboard side was much lower than the shothole where they struck on the port side. But the shots of the *Sydney* went straight through the *Emden*, the hole of exit being practically on the same level as the entry. Such an advantage do heavier naval guns give in a duel at sea.

The fourth shot of the *Emden* was a good hit; it went through the *Sydney's* deck and exploded below, wounding Petty Officer Harvey and another man. An Australian lad who was detailed there to watch for torpedoes never even turned round at the explosion, nor did he move the telescope from his eyes. At the same time the *Sydney* was scoring hits on the *Emden*, though the first sign of it to the Australians was not observable until the fall of one of the German's funnels, which was greeted with loud cheering from all the *Sydney's* company. A minute afterwards the foremast of the raider toppled over, carrying with it the main fire control, and throwing its members into the sea.

When fighting had been in progress for a quarter of an hour the *Sydney* discharged a salvo which settled any hope the Germans may have cherished either of victory or escape. It entered the *Emden's* stern under the afterdeck, where it burst, blowing up the whole of the steel deck. The steel plates were twisted and shattered beyond anything that could have been deemed possible; the after gun was dismounted, and the crew blown into the sea; the ship was set afire aft, and remained afire for the rest of the fight. Most serious effect of all, the salvo destroyed the steering gear, and for the rest of the battle the *Emden* had to steer by means of her screw, thus reducing her speed immensely, and leaving her completely at the mercy of the manœuvres of her opponent.

The *Emden* now swung round, doubling in an attempt to reduce the distance; but the *Sydney* easily countered the move by following the operation; and continued steaming parallel with the German, and battering her to pieces. In the first quarter of an hour, and before she had received her deadly injury, the *Emden* had scored several important hits on the *Sydney*. One had struck the second starboard gun, and set fire to some cordite, which the gun crew threw overboard. This shot was followed by a shrapnel shell in the same quarter, which killed two of the gun's crew and injured all the rest except two. Another shot exploded in the lads' room, and damaged their kits; but the room was empty, and no one was hurt.

But after that explosion aft she never struck the *Sydney* again, though the fight lasted for an hour longer. She had been firing with remarkable speed; it is believed that the third salvo was out of her guns sometimes ere the first had reached the neighbourhood of the *Sydney*. In all she fired

1,400 shots, of which only ten struck their mark; and of these only three, or at the most four, could be considered important hits.

Again she doubled, with smoke pouring from her at every quarter. Suddenly the whole company of the *Sydney* burst into ringing cheers. "She's gone," was the shout; and indeed for a time it appeared as though the *Emden* had suddenly gone down. Reports from the centre of a patch of curiously light-coloured smoke dissipated the notion; the *Emden* was still afloat, and still fighting. The smoke that hid her was the smoke that showed how badly she was hurt. One by one her guns ceased firing, as the well-directed shots from the *Sydney* put them out of action; but still she ran, and still she fought her remaining guns.

One by one her funnels collapsed, and fell across the twisted deck. Only one gun was left, a gun far forward on the port side. Desperately the crippled *Emden* ran, and desperately she fought her last little gun. What an inferno she then was, only those who fought her can tell. Her gnarled steel work was hot with the raging fire; the smoke from her furnaces belched from the holes left by the fallen funnels, and streamed in scorching clouds across her deck. Her ammunition hoists, and most of the rest of her equipment, had been hopelessly damaged; and what ammunition was being used had to be carried to her remaining gun by hand. The ship was a shambles, with dead men lying everywhere, and badly wounded as well. But in the conning tower Captain von Mueller still fought his ship, and prayed for a shot to carry him and it away.

His ship was wrapped in flame; the stern actually glowing red hot with the fire. She no longer could be steered, even by the employment of her screws; and with her ensign still flying, and her solitary gun roaring at intervals, she ran high up on the coral reef, a hopeless, shattered wreck. Her conqueror gave her two broadsides as she lay there, with her bow high out of the water and only a short stretch of surf between her and dry land. Her ensign was still flying, and Captain Glossop had to make sure.

While the fight was in progress a merchant ship had hovered round the combatants; obviously most anxious as to the result of the duel. At one period she showed signs of wishing to take part with the *Emden*, and the guns of the *Sydney* had been trained upon her, though no shot was fired at her. She was really a collier which had been captured by the *Emden*, and with a prize crew from the *Emden* on board had met the raider at Cocos Island. Her crew had considered the advisability of trying to ram the *Sydney*, but were wise enough to abandon the scheme, and make for safety when the fight went so badly against their side.

When the *Emden* ran ashore this collier was already a long distance away; in fact she was almost out of sight. The *Sydney* put after her, and after a long chase came near enough to send a shot across her bows as a summons to surrender. She was boarded, but by this time she was sinking, as some one on board had turned on the seacocks, and filled her with water. The crew was accordingly taken off her, and she was abandoned to her fate, the *Sydney* returning to the *Emden*.

The tide had gone out, and the one-time terror to the commerce of the British Empire was lying high and dry, with her ensign still floating. "Do you surrender?" signalled the Australian warship. To this question the *Emden* replied by hand signal: "We have lost our book, and cannot make out your signal." Then Captain Glossop sent the curt demand, "Haul down your ensign." As the Germans paid no attention to this, he sent yet another message, intimating that he would resume hostilities if the ensign were not hauled down in twenty minutes. For so long he steamed up and down her stern, while the white flag with the black cross still fluttered upon the wreck Then reluctantly, and because he had no option, Captain Glossop fired three more salvos at the defiant raider. Down came the German ensign and in its place the white flag of surrender was hoisted.

Those three last salvos, unwillingly discharged at short range into a helpless hull, did terrible havoc. The scorching decks were strewn with dead and wounded sailors, hapless victims to a tradition the Kaiser has sought to impose upon a navy that has no traditions of its own making. The *Sydney* could not succour them yet, for there was still work left for her to do. A boat manned by the German prize crew of the collier was sent to the wreck, with the message that the *Sydney* would return to the assistance of those on board early in the morning.

It is now necessary to relate what occurred upon the island, where we left the British and Germans together gazing spellbound at the opening of this remarkable ocean duel. After the deadly salvo which crippled the *Emden* had been fired, the German landing party recognized that their ship was doomed. They at once ordered the British off the roof of the cable station, and shut them up in a room where they could not know what was going on. They behaved courteously but firmly, taking every precaution that there should be no interference with the work now before them. There was lying at the island the schooner *Ayesha*, and into this vessel they loaded everything they could find that was likely to be useful for a long ocean voyage.

By the middle of the afternoon they were all ready, and about half an hour before the *Sydney* returned from her chase of the collier they set sail, taking with them the three boats and four maxim guns with which they had landed They were about forty in number, and their bold plan of escape was successful. The story of their adventures on the little schooner is a romance in itself; it belongs to the history that Germany will one day produce of the daring of her own men. Before leaving, they had done all the damage they could to the cable and wireless stations.

Next morning the *Sydney* returned to the wreck, taking with her the doctor from Cocos Island, and all the helpers that could be mustered. The *Emden* was found in a condition truly pitiful. The deck was a tangle of twisted steel; so shattered that it was impossible to make a way about it. The survivors were huddled together in the forecastle, the only part of the ship which had not been made an inferno by the fire, which was still burning aft, and had scorched the stern out of all shape or even existence. There was not a drop of fresh water on the ship, and the food supplies were inaccessible or destroyed. For quite twenty-four hours the survivors, many of them suffering from terrible wounds, had been without food or even drink.

To reach the shore was a matter almost of impossibility, so heavy was the sea that was running. To make matters worse, the more experienced of the two doctors carried by the German cruiser had had his thigh broken in the action. In their despair some of the crew, including a number of wounded men, had managed to reach the shore, only to be mocked by a waterless and utterly barren patch of sand.

The work of rescue was a difficult business. Only four or five wounded men could be taken off by each boat; and the company of the *Sydney* worked hard all day at their task. Night fell with it still unaccomplished, but it was completed on the following day. Each wounded man meant a hard task, the work of getting the injured on the boats, and hoisting them from the boats on to the *Sydney*, being complicated by the roughness of the sea, and the dreadful injuries and sufferings they had one and all experienced.

The losses on both sides showed how utterly the *Emden* was outfought. The *Sydney* lost three men killed outright, while one more afterwards died of his wounds. Four were seriously wounded, four more were returned as wounded, and yet another four as slightly wounded. The men killed were : Petty Officer Thomas Lynch, Able Seamen Albert Hoy and Reginald Sharpe, and Ordinary Seaman Robert Bell.

The *Emden* lost, in the action and by drowning,

twelve officers and 119 men ; the prisoners totalled eleven officers, nine warrant officers, and 191 men. Of these three officers and fifty-three men were wounded, most of them seriously. The fight lasted for an hour and forty minutes, though after the first fifteen minutes the battle was a hopeless one for the Germans. In their manœuvres the combatant vessels covered more than thirty miles during the progress of the fight.

Every courtesy was extended to the prisoners ; the officers were allowed to keep their swords, and were treated by the Australians with such consideration as their refusal to give parole permitted. The wounded were tended with the utmost solicitude, and repaid the care lavished on them with expressions of the liveliest gratitude.

The *Sydney* rejoined her convoy at Colombo, one of the world's great ports of call. The great roadstead was swarming with friendly vessels, the city lay white above the cliffs of Galle Face, the houses nestling among the brilliant green of the palms, bisected with startling red roads. Above, a cloudless blue sky, and the British flag proudly floating over all. Colombo is one of those " places in the sun " which have aroused the covetous greed of his Majesty Wilhelm II.

The flagship *Melbourne* signalled her course to the *Sydney*, and the victorious cruiser swung round and steamed between the long rows of transports.

The side of each swarmed with Australasian soldiers, all greeting the conqueror, hat in hand. The silence was so oppressive that the captured Germans looked uneasily at one another. Every ship in the harbour showed its bunting, but no whistle blew, no cheer was raised to greet the heroes of the fight.

Piqued into an unrestrainable curiosity by this apparent lack of emotion, one of the German captured officers asked an officer of the *Sydney* why there was no cheering. He was told, very simply, that as there were prisoners on the cruiser, suffering from serious wounds gallantly sustained, the *Sydney* had sent a message asking that no noisy demonstration should mark her return to the fleet. This reply unmanned him completely. With tears in his eyes he said, "You have been kind, but this crowns all; we cannot speak to thank you for it."

For Australians not the least proud of the memories of the first engagement fought by their navy will ever be that silent greeting of the returning conqueror. The restraint imposed upon that army of Australasians, going out for the first time to make war in Europe, was hardly natural, when the thrilling nature of the incident is considered. The chivalrous care for the wounded enemy will surely immortalize the gallant sailors who desired it, and the brave soldiers who respected their wish so thoroughly.

But elsewhere such restraint was not necessary. On November 10, the news of the destruction of the *Emden* was announced at Lloyd's in London, the parting knell of the raider being rung on the bell of the old *Lutine*. The underwriters, mindful of the £2,500,000 of damage done by the raider to British commerce, burst spontaneously into hearty cheering for the *Sydney* and her bold crew ; also for the newest navy in the world, the navy of the Commonwealth of Australia.

From all parts of the world messages of congratulation were flashed to the Prime Minister of Australia. For the first time the man in the street realized that Australia really had a navy, efficient in the highest degree as to quality, though still limited in the number of its component vessels.

IN THE LAND OF PHARAOH

CHAPTER III

IN THE LAND OF PHARAOH

THE fight that ended in the destruction of the *Emden* was the one exciting incident that broke the monotony of the tedious voyage from Australia. When they had left Albany, the last port of call in Australia, the men believed that they would go to Great Britain, there to train for service in Northern France. The intervention of Turkey in the war on the side of the Teutonic nations caused the original intention to be altered, and the men heard that they were to disembark at Egypt. This decision shortened the voyage originally undertaken by nearly one-half, but delays, especially at the Suez Canal, made the journey still a long one. The men who shipped in Tasmania spent nine weeks on the transports before finally disembarking in Egypt; while some of the New Zealanders had even a longer spell of troopship life.

All were glad, therefore, for the break in the monotony afforded by the *Emden* incident; for the whole fleet witnessed the sudden dash of the *Sydney* at break-neck speed, and shared the glad news flashed by the cruiser by wireless, that reached the convoy some six hours later. The one menace to the safety of the convoy was thus removed, and the remainder of the journey was devoid even of the interest arising out of the possibility of attack. All were correspondingly pleased when they left the transports and entered their Egyptian camps; the Australians at Mena in the shadow of the Pyramids, and the New Zealanders at Heliopolis.

It is doubtful whether the good people of Cairo have quite yet got over the surprise occasioned them by the proceedings of our Australasian army during their first few days in residence in Egypt. The men certainly behaved as no soldiers had ever behaved before, in Egypt's fairly wide experience. They were as unlike the traditional Mr. Atkins of the British regular army—the type to which Cairo has been accustomed—as it is possible for men of the same race to be. They were young men just freed from the restrictions of life on a troopship; many of them had plenty of money to spend; few of them had ever called any man master, or been subject to any will but their own.

Their frame of mind was well understood by those in control of them; and for the first few days a good deal of latitude was allowed the newly-

The Australians returning to Camp at Mena, in Egypt.

landed Australasians. In those few days the word went round the bazaars that all the Australasians were surely millionaires ; and that many of them were many times madder than the mad English. Taxicabs (at two shillings an hour) became unattainable things each evening in Cairo ; they were monopolized by Australasian private soldiers seeing the sights.

They went into camp on December 8, at the very height of the Egyptian season. A night or two later, a table was set in the most prominent part of the dining-room of one of Cairo's costliest and most fashionable hotels. The place was crowded, and many visitors sought in vain for seats at dinner ; this table was exclusively guarded by an unapproachable waiter, who averred that it had been set aside for a party of most particular gentlemen. Presently these gentlemen arrived, all attired in the uniforms of privates in the Australian army, and to the scandal of some of those present proceeded to enjoy, cheerfully but decorously, the best the house could produce.

One dragoman of Cairo was accosted by an Australian private, who engaged his services, explaining that he wished to buy carpets to send to Australia as presents to his friends there. The dragoman, wishing to overawe him by a display of the unattainable, took him to a merchant who exhibited three carpets as a beginning, one of which cost

£100, and the other two £75 each. While the dragoman was explaining to the seller of carpets that his would-be customer was but a private soldier, and only able to buy very cheap goods, the Australian produced the cash for all three carpets, and leaving an address to which they were to be sent, strolled off. This case is but one of many incidents which excited the keen merchants of Egypt, and gave rise to the bazaar talk of the unlimited wealth of these Australians, even those who served in the ranks.

From Cairo to the Pyramids there runs a thin asphalt road, bordered by green irrigation patches and sandy wastes of desert. Each night in those first easy weeks in Egypt, this road was thronged at midnight by all the motley vehicles Cairo could produce, all crammed with happy soldiers returning to camp after a night's fun in the city. Every day the sights of the neighbourhood were visited by scores of curious Australasians; the desire to climb to the top of the great pyramid of Cheops consumed them; no less than seven men fell in attempting it. Four of them were killed outright, and another was maimed for life.

The wisdom of affording them an outlet for their high spirits was apparent when, a week or so after landing, the work of military training began in earnest. One and all, they settled down to the collar like veterans, and soon twenty-mile

Australian Soldiers at the Foot of the Pyramids.

marches through the heavy sand became a joke, as battalion vied with battalion in breaking records of physical fitness. "Physically, they are the finest lot of men I have ever seen in any part of the world," wrote Mr. Ashmead Bartlett, when they came under his observation at this period in their training. At the end of the year both Australians and New Zealanders were able to show at reviews how much they had already benefited by their training.

The occasion of these reviews was the visit to Egypt of Sir George Reid and the Hon. Thomas McKenzie, the High Commissioners in London for the Commonwealth of Australia and the Dominion of New Zealand respectively. The Australians were reviewed at Mena, and the New Zealanders at Heliopolis; and at both reviews General Sir John Maxwell, the officer commanding his Majesty's troops in Egypt, was present. He asked the High Commissioner to convey to the Commonwealth Government his congratulations upon the superb appearance of the Australians. The New Zealanders, with their continuous lines of six feet men, drew from him the observation, "It would be impossible to obtain better material anywhere."

The men were much pleased with the visits of their London representatives, and cheered them to the echo when they departed. Before leaving, Sir George Reid addressed the following letter to the Australians composing the expeditionary force :—

"General Bridges, Officers, Non-commissioned Officers, and men of the Australian Imperial force:
"Gentlemen,—

"My visit to Egypt to welcome you at this stage of your journey to the front has been crowded with interesting events. The ancient glories— the new and beneficent Protectorate—the accession to the throne of a wise and enlightened Sultan ; a state of martial law, most necessary as a precaution, but without any trace of hardship, severity, or discontent—all these unique events have made my short stay in Egypt unsurpassingly interesting.

"But, standing out above all, is the delight with which I have seen you, the representatives of the manhood and loyalty of the Australian Commonwealth. If, to an old Australian like myself, you have excelled every other display of manhood I have ever seen, you can imagine the impression you have made upon others. But the youth and lack of experience in warlike operations of most of you reminds me always that, after all, you are as yet only the raw material out of which efficient soldiers have to be made. To become worthy of the first rank in the most bloody, desperate and scientific war from which the world has ever suffered, you must begin by a conquest

Sir George Reid, High Commissioner for the Commonwealth, reviewing the Australian Expeditionary Force at Mena Camp, Egypt.

of self, by cheerful and constant and absolute submission to authority, to the authority of the corporal just as implicitly as that of the General Orders. If you are to retain the good opinion you have already won, you must achieve wonders of discipline and hard work. You must observe rigid rules of conduct, you must excel in devotion to duty. The ability and patriotism of Australian statesmen of all parties—of the whole Parliament —and of the Australian people, have chosen you wisely, and equipped you splendidly ; the rest is in your hands. Prepared to risk, and sacrifice if it must be so, your lives, back up your noble resolve by a supreme effort to develop your efficiency and stamina of body and soul to the highest point. Acting thus in life you will triumph, and in death, you will triumph also. Remember• the liberties of mankind are involved just as deeply as the name and fame and welfare of Australia.

"Hoping to see the forces in London crowned with laurels of victory,

"Most faithfully yours
"G. H. REID,
"*High Commissioner.*
"CAIRO, *January* 11, 1915."

The next two months were months of hard work. Twenty-mile marches through the desert sand with a 70-lb. load took all the desire for an evening's fun in Cairo out of even the friskiest of them, and in surprisingly short time they settled down into soldiers as good as they looked—steady, resourceful and disciplined, as they were soon to prove on one of the bloodiest battlefields of the Great War.

For some of them the baptism of fire came in Egypt, when the Turks made their farcical attempt on the Suez Canal. The New Zealand Infantry and the Australian Engineers took part in the engagement which ended that attempt, and comported themselves well. The New Zealanders captured one of the celebrated galvanized iron boats, which the Turks had lugged across the desert for the crossing of the canal, and it was sent to New Zealand, the first trophy of the war from the Old World for Australasia.

Training in Egypt continued till early in April, and then a large proportion of the Australasians were despatched to the Dardanelles, to assist in the attempt to force the passage of the Straits, already begun by the combined British and French fleets. The first task before the Expeditionary Force to the Dardanelles was to effect a landing on the Gallipoli Peninsula.

THE BATTLE OF BRIGHTON BEACH

CHAPTER IV

THE BATTLE OF BRIGHTON BEACH

FOUR months in camp under the passionless gaze of the great Sphinx had shaken the men into a thoroughly fit and efficient army. It had also wearied them into an ardent desire to be up and doing. Each day brought them news of the fierce fighting in Belgium and Northern France. Their cousins and friendly rivals from Canada had already won undying glory, and the Australasians chafed at the monotonous round of hard work and military discipline that seemed to lead to nothing. Not for this had they come half-way across the world; they yearned to be in the thick of it, and show how they could fight for the Empire they were so proud to serve.

The glad excitement that followed the announcement that they were detailed for active and immediate service can well be imagined; and additional joy was displayed when it became known that they were to serve on the classic battleground that borders the Dardanelles. And indeed, there is something of the miraculous in the dispatch of this composite army from two nations that dwell where a century and a half ago no white man existed to the scene of the first great adventure recorded in written history : the quest of the Golden Fleece.

Their land of the Golden Fleece lay thousands of miles away, still unscarred by any war, whatever the future may hold for it. Many of them, until they embarked on this momentous expedition, had never seen any other lands than their own. They had read of the adventures of Homer's heroes, but the scene of those exploits might as well have been laid in some other planet, for all the conception they could form of it. They knew that Alexander the Great had crossed the Dardanelles with a force no greater than their own, and had returned as Conqueror of Asia. For thousands of years the possession of those few miles of narrow sea passage had been the subject of contention among nations that had passed away for ever. Now they, the first real army of the newest nations, came to dispute its possession with an old and decadent race, which for hundreds of years had terrorized Eastern Europe.

Yes, these sheep-farmers and fruit-growers, these land agents and miners and city clerks, were the new Argonauts. They had left the Golden Fleece behind them, and the peaceful sunlit plains of Australia. They had deserted the wind-swept heights of New Zealand, where the salt breeze fans the cheek, and the snow-clad summits of the mountains are mirrored in the placid bosoms of lakes more beautiful than any the Old World has ever seen. Their quest was honour for themselves and the young races they represented ; they went to fight for justice, for the unity of the Empire, for the cause of the weak and small nations of Europe. Surely their dispatch to the Dardanelles ranks with the greatest of great adventures.

The whole of the Dardanelles Expedition was commanded by General Sir Ian Hamilton, a familiar name and figure to Australasians, since he was instrumental, by his report on the state of the Australasian defence forces, and by his recommendations, in the establishment of the system of compulsory military training in vogue throughout Australasia. Sir Ian Hamilton's plans provided for a number of separate but simultaneous landings on the peninsula of Gallipoli ; and, as a blind, a landing by the French troops which formed a component part of the force at his disposal, on the Asiatic shore of the Dardanelles. Owing to the strong fortifications and defences which had been contrived by the Turks upon plans of German origin, the task of effecting a landing was an extremely difficult one ; von der Goltz, the German general who had designed the defences, boasted that it was impossible of accomplishment. His boast, like that of the *Emden's* captain, was soon to be proved an empty and vainglorious one.

The place chosen for the landing of the Australasians was Gaba Tepe, a high point on the Gulf of Saros, opposite the town of Maidos on the Straits. It should be pointed out here that the landing of troops at this point was of the highest strategical importance, as the presence of a hostile force there would be a continual menace to the Turkish communications. A successful advance of such a force would drive a wedge between the strong forts at the Narrows, on which the attack of the Allies was concentrated, and the Turkish base at Constantinople.

The actual landing party was the Third Australian Brigade, a mixed body of men from Queensland, South Australia and West Australia, commanded by Colonel Sinclair Maclagan, D.S.O. These men 1,500 in number, embarked at Mudros Bay on April 24 on British battleships, and set out for Gaba Tepe. Following them were the men of the 1st and 2nd Brigades, a covering force of 2,500. These were conveyed to the landing place in transports. The reason of embarking the actual landing force in warships was fairly obvious. It was hoped that a landing on the rough and inaccessible spot chosen for the Australasians might be effected unopposed ; and it was argued that the Turks, who might have been alarmed at the sight of transports and so have time to prepare an opposing force, would accept the presence of warships as merely the

Transports bearing the Australasians to Anzac Cove.

prelude to one of the bombardments to which they were now accustomed.

As a matter of fact, the British plans were not hidden from the enemy, for the place actually chosen for the landing was afterwards discovered to have been elaborately prepared for resistance. Barbed wire was entangled under the water, and the beach was enfiladed with machine guns. The cliff was honeycombed with hiding places for snipers, and only a fortunate accident saved the Australians from a much hotter reception than the very warm one accorded them by the Turks.

The landing force arrived opposite Gaba Tepe at 1.30 a.m., and the men were transferred in absolute silence to their boats. At the same time the covering force was transhipped from the transports to six destroyers ; and all made for a point about four miles off the coast. The dying moon rose as they steamed to this place, and the outlines of the ships were visible to the Turks, who were watching from the shore. At half-past three the landing force was ordered to go forward, and the tows made for the land with all dispatch.

Now occurred the happy accident to which allusion has already been made. The tows got off the line they had intended to take, and reached the beach about a mile north of the spot actually selected for the landing. A description of the landing place, which will go down to history as Brighton Beach, is given by Sir Ian Hamilton in his first official dispatch of the operations at the Dardanelles.

"The beach on which the landing was actually effected is a very narrow strip of sand, about 1,000 yards in length, bounded on the north and the south by two small promontories. At its southern extremity a deep ravine, with exceedingly steep, scrub-clad sides, runs inland in a north-easterly direction. Near the northern end of the beach a small but steep gully runs up into the hills at right angles to the shore.

"Between the ravine and the gully the whole of the beach is backed by the seaward face of the spur which forms the north-western side of the ravine. From the top of the spur the ground falls almost sheer, except near the southern limit of the beach, where gentler slopes give access to the mouth of the ravine behind. Further inland lie in a tangled knot the under-features of Sari Bair, separated by deep ravines, which take a most confusing diversity of direction. Sharp spurs, covered with dense scrub, and falling away in many places in precipitous sandy cliffs, radiate from the principal mass of the mountain, from which they run north-west, west, south-west, and south to the coast."

Obeying orders to the letter, the Australians sat as quiet as mice in the boats as the tows neared the land; on the edge of the cliffs they could see the Turks scampering along at breakneck speed, to be in the right place to receive them. And now the boats were nearing the shore, and a new sensation was provided for the men of Australia.

"You know one of those hot days when a storm blows up in Australia," said one of the party, in describing it. "The air seems heavy, as if there was lead in it. Then, splash! All around you on the pavement appear big drops, that hit the asphalt with a welt. Well, all of a sudden something began to hit the water all round us just like that. We knew from the rattle on the shore what it was. Bullets! A man two places away from me sank quietly on the bottom of the boat; something touched my hat and ruffled my hair. We were under hot fire for a start."

As the boats reached the shallow water the Australians jumped in up to the waist, and made for the sand; some of them died in the moment their feet first touched Europe. "Like lightning," writes General Sir Ian Hamilton, in his official dispatch, describing the landing, "the Australians, leapt ashore, and each man as he did so went straight as his bayonet at the enemy. So vigorous was the onslaught that the Turks made no attempt to withstand it, and fled from ridge to ridge pursued by the Australian infantry."

It must be remembered that the cliff up which this bayonet charge was made was from 30 to 50 feet high, and as described by Sir Ian Hamilton, was "almost sheer." At each end of the strip of beach was a higher knoll, about a hundred feet in height. On each of these were posted scores of sharpshooters, who were firing as rapidly as they could at the men scrambling up these cliffs; the Turks at the top could not even fire at them, the cliffs were so steep.

As the men sprang from the boats they set off in groups of five or six, acting on their own initiative. They had empty magazines, all the work being left to the cold steel. In that terrible scramble up the cliffside they fell by dozens, but the rest pressed on to the trenches at the top. The Turks who waited for them there had to encounter infuriated giants. One Australian still bears the name of "The Haymaker," for his way of picking Turk after Turk on the end of his bayonet and throwing them one after another over his shoulder and over the edge of the cliff behind. Two or three more great men preferred to use the butt, smashing down everything human that dared to resist them. In a few moments the Turks had abandoned their trenches and were flying up the foothills to another trench they had prepared on the top of a ridge.

Fast as they ran, the Australians ran faster. The cries of "Come on, Australians," rang through the ravines, and warned the Turks ahead of their coming. The first ridge was occupied, and a second; finally they reached a third nearly two miles inland.

The Landing at Anzac Cove on Sunday, April 25, 1915.

It must be understood that they had waited for no orders and had not tarried for any formation. Men of different battalions and from different States swept forward together, all acting on their own initiative, and all prepared to sacrifice themselves for the main object, which was to clear the clifftops so as to permit of a safe landing for the main body of the troops. These watched the fighting in the lightening morning from the decks of the ships, while waiting their turn to land.

They could see on one ridge after another the gaunt figures of their comrades appear, only to disappear over the crest, presently to become visible yet farther inland. How they cheered as the pioneers swept the Turks off the coast and drove them into the thick scrub that skirted the more distant ranges of hills! The audacity of that landing has no superior in history, and Australian soldiers will ever be remembered for their initiative, resource, and daring. Where men less used to acting on their own responsibility would have formed bravely, and waited for orders from some superior, these men from the South dashed off in little groups, all working efficiently, as if by some tacit understanding.

So the 3rd Brigade cleared the way for the 1st and 2nd Brigades, so that 12,000 infantry and two batteries of Indian mountain guns were landed by two o'clock—smart work on such a difficult coast in ten hours. For this splendid record the greatest credit is due to the Navy men, of whom the Australasians all speak as they would of the greatest heroes on earth. Their coolness, their unassuming courage, and their steadfast adherence to the object in view are topics of which Australians who were there will never tire of talking. And the men of the Navy have an equally high opinion of those law bushmen whom they set down on that narrow strip of bullet-swept beach.

For it must not be supposed that the clearance of the trenches opposite the landing place made the task of landing in any way a safe one. All day long batteries posted in the hills, which had the range of the beach quite accurately, continued to spray the landing with shrapnel. One sandy point was christened by the Australians Hellfire Spit, and will go down to history by that name. Their name for the landing place was Brighton Beach, which name it now bears on the official maps. British people must not suppose that this name has any reference to the seaside town which is sometimes called London-by-the-Sea. The Australians had in mind another Brighton, 12,000 miles away, where the cliffs rise abruptly from a sandy beach, and where the eye rests on slopes covered with a thick growth of scrubby ti-tree, of which the scrub on the hillsides at Gaba Tepe reminded the men of Australia. So it is Brighton Beach near

Melbourne, and not Brighton Beach in Sussex, that gave its name to the landing place at Gaba Tepe.

There were also guns on each of the two knolls which terminated Brighton Beach, and from them and from machine guns very cleverly placed on high points a cruel enfilading fire was directed upon the beach. The guns on the knolls were one by one put out of action by the warships, but some of the machine guns, as well as innumerable snipers, continued to fire on the boats and on the landed men throughout the day. Many a brave Australasian met a bullet before ever he set foot on the soil of Europe, and the sailors suffered heavily but doggedly as they rowed their boats to and fro between the ships and the landing place.

It is now necessary to follow the fortunes of the little bands of the gallant 3rd Brigade, whose rush had carried them over three successive ridges on to a high tableland, where the backs of the retreating Turks were still visible. "Where's the Light Horse?" the men shouted as they rushed on in pursuit. The Light Horse was then eating out its heart somewhere in Egypt, wishing that such an animal as the horse had never been created, and that they might be with their comrades of the infantry, fighting in Australasia's first great battle. Of course they could never have got cavalry up on to that plateau, though mounted men would have been very useful when the first Australian soldiers crossed the ridges, and reached its wide, scrubby slopes.

These devoted little bands found more than stragglers on that high plateau. Soon the advance guard of the main Turkish defence force arrived on the scene, and then it went very badly with these bold spirits. The fate of many of those little groups of brave, resourceful soldiers is yet to be learned; most of them appear on the sheets as "Missing." Those behind them were thrown back by sheer force of numbers, as the main body of the Turks pressed on, and fighting gallantly, fell back on the second line.

By nightfall the main body of the Australians, all mixed up just as they had landed, and without regard to battalions or anything else, was dug in on the clifftop, and fighting desperately to prevent the Turks from dislodging them.

"The troops had had no rest on the night of the 24th-25th," writes the General, "they had been fighting hard all day over most difficult country, and they had been subjected to heavy shrapnel fire in the open. Their casualties had been deplorably heavy. But despite their losses and in spite of their fatigue, the morning of the 26th found them still in good heart, and as full of fight as ever."

Such is the story of the battle of Brighton Beach, ending with our boys "in good heart, and full of fight as ever." The wounded and dying men were

Shrapnel bursting over Anzac Cove.

also in good heart. Mr. Ashmead Bartlett describes the arrival of the first batch of Australian wounded back to the ships in a passage that will stir every Australian's pulse till the very end of time.

"I have never seen the like of these wounded Australians in war before, for as they were towed among the ships while accommodation was being found for them, although many of them were shot to bits and without hope of recovery, their cheers resounded through the night, and you could just see amid a mass of suffering humanity arms being waved in greeting to the crews of the warships. They were happy because they knew they had been tried for the first time in the war, and had not been found wanting. They had been told to occupy the heights and hold on, and this they had done for fifteen mortal hours under an incessant shell fire without the moral and material support of a single gun ashore, and subjected the whole time to the violent counter-attacks of a brave enemy led by skilful leaders, while his snipers, hidden in caves, thickets, and among the dense scrub, made a deliberate practice of picking off every officer who endeavoured to give a word of command or to lead his men forward.

"No finer feat of arms has been performed during the war than this sudden landing in the dark, this storming of the heights, and, above all, the holding on to the points thus won while reinforcements were being poured from the transports. These raw Colonial troops in those desperate hours proved themselves worthy to fight side by side with the heroes of Mons and the Aisne, Ypres and Neuve Chapelle."

OCCUPYING THE LAND

CHAPTER V

OCCUPYING THE LAND

THE morning of April 26 found the Australasians occupying the clifftop in a long semicircle, with its right resting on the sea at a point opposite the hill of Gaba Tepe, and the left resting on high ground above the coast at a place called Fisherman's Hut. The New Zealanders were on the extreme left, with the 4th Australian Brigade in support of them; next were the 1st Brigade from New South Wales, next to them were the 2nd Brigade of men from Victoria, while on the right were the 3rd Brigade, or what was left of it.

All night they had been fighting, the Turks making brave but ineffectual attempts to dislodge them, and being quite unable to prevent them from digging themselves in. The scattered groups of pioneers were soon sorted out into their various battalions, missing men turned up from all sorts of unexpected places, and order was rapidly instituted among the ranks. This was a very necessary step, for men had been fighting side by side with perfect strangers, a state of things which afforded unlimited opportunities to the host of spies and snipers who swarmed boldly among the Australians, and, employing perfect English, did much to create confusion and loss among them.

Some incidents that occurred during that temporary confusion are evidence of the amazing audacity of these enemies, most of whom were Germans. They were equipped with undeniable Australian uniforms, and spoke with the same accent as the average Australian officer. One of these fellows encountered Captain Macdonald and Lieutenant Elston, of the 16th Battalion (West Australia), and professed to convey to them orders from a superior officer that they should at once go to a spot beyond a piece of rising ground. Unsuspectingly they went, and fell into the hands of a band of Turks, who made them prisoners. The same man delivered a similar message to Colonel Pope, also of West Australia, but on his way to the rendezvous this officer saw something which made him suspicious. He took a flying leap from the rise on which he was walking into a patch of soft sand many feet below, and just in time to save his life. The rise where this took place was promptly christened Pope's Hill; it lies to the left of the deep ravine mentioned in Sir Ian Hamilton's dispatch as being one of the main features of the ground before the Australian line.

The enemy had also become acquainted with

the Australian bugle calls, and in the darkness the "Retire" was frequently sounded on the bugle, loudly and insistently. But before landing the precaution had been taken to announce that all bugles had been removed, and that other signals had been substituted. Consequently no notice was taken of this ruse on the part of the enemy, except that it made the Australians profoundly suspicious. And when their suspicions were aroused, the Australians were not easily duped, as many a bold spy found to his cost.

One fellow, in the dress of an Australian officer, ventured to convey some spurious orders to a small group of men who were holding a detached position. He was heard with a show of respect, and then the sergeant asked, "What battalion is yours, sir?" "The 22nd" was the ready reply; a very good one, if there had been a 22nd battalion. "And what ship did you cross on?" continued the questioner. "There is no need to cross-examine your superior officer" was the answer, delivered with the utmost coolness. Just then a rifle cracked, and the supposed officer spun round and fell. "Bit sudden, aren't you?" asked the sergeant of the gaunt Australian who strode forward. "What?" said the shooter, "22nd battalion! Don't know what ship he came on! Let's look at his papers." There was found plenty of proof that the summary methods of the bush were fully justified; and the example was a wholesome one for the audacious colleagues the spy undoubtedly possessed, who had found their way among the temporarily disorganized Australasians.

The snipers, with whom the hillsides were thick, showed in some instances an equal audacity, leaving their prepared hiding places in the scrub on the approach of the Australians, and joining with them in the dusk, pretending to help them look for snipers. During the first few days these marksmen accounted for many brave Australian officers, and in some instances it has been established that an Australian officer was killed by a shot fired from behind, the sniper's lair being passed by the advancing line, though that line contained many bushmen of great skill and experience.

On the other hand, a great number of these fellows were tracked to their hiding places, where they thought themselves quite safe, and got short shrift. The nature of the country made all these ruses possible to the Turks and their German tutors. Most of it was covered with a dense scrub of short, bushy trees, with branches growing right down to the ground. Set very close together, these afforded excellent cover to both sides, but the initial advantage lay, of course, with the defenders, especially in the early days before the Australasians had become familiar with the country. An instance of the density of this scrub is given by an officer of high rank, who, on a tour of inspection, found a group of some twenty soldiers advancing cautiously through the thickest of it. On asking them how they were progressing, he was told, with a great show of genuine sorrow, that they were the survivors of over a hundred, the rest having been cut off. He was able to tell the " survivors " that they were the third group he had encountered in his tour, each believing that the others were hopelessly cut off by the enemy.

In that first twenty-four hours of fighting the Australasian officers set an example of cool courage and hardihood that might have spurred men less daring than their own to deeds of the greatest courage. " The officers were splendid " is the universal verdict of the men, who are not easily moved to enthusiasm. But Australia and New Zealand paid a heavy toll of their finest officers and most trusted leaders. The first man out of the boats was Major Gordon, of Queensland, who leaped into the water shoulder high, followed by a dozen brave fellows in the same instant. But a bullet cut the gallant Major off before he set foot on dry land, the first Australian officer to give up his life in Gallipoli. In the very act of landing Major Robertson, of Queensland, fell dead; Colonel Braund and Colonel Garside did not long outlive him, nor did Colonel Clarke.

Next day saw the death of Colonel McLaurin,

one of the leading barristers at the Sydney bar, and a man whose high character was renowned from one end to the other of Australia. "He was a man of singularly high, noble and chivalrous mind," wrote one who knew him well, when his death was announced. "No unworthy word ever passed his lips; it was impossible to imagine any action of his that would be other than generous and just; and there is no doubt that with his remarkable abilities, his courage, and his charm of character, he would have attained the highest position in his profession, or in the profession of arms."

An equally high value was rightly placed by Australia and New Zealand upon other of their brave citizen soldiers who perished gallantly in that first day's fighting so far from home. With simple emotion a West Australian Sergeant tells of the death of the brave Colonel Clarke. "We stormed the cliff, and the Turks did not wait for us. Halfway up I came across our Colonel. He had his pack on. I asked him to throw it down, but he said that he did not want to lose it, so I carried it for him. We advanced about one mile and a half due east of our landing-place, and found the Turks holding a ridge in great strength, so we lay down and opened fire. I was alongside the Colonel, and had just given him his pack and got down again, when *zip*—a bullet got him in the body. He was dead in a minute. Major Elliott was sent for.

He had been there only two seconds when he was hit. Another officer came up and he was hit, so we had got into a fairly hot place."

The difficult country made it necessary that officers should take great risks when making observations, and they took them cheerfully and courageously. The casualty lists show what a heavy penalty was paid in officers killed and wounded, but the success attending the operations proves that the risk and the loss was not without fruit. Those lives, so cheerfully risked and lost, were not wasted; they were spent audaciously for the purpose in view. " You cannot lead your men from the rear," was the motto of the Australasian officers at Gaba Tepe, and disregarding the imploring counsel of the men beside them they set an example that Australasia will ever mourn and cherish.

The rewards for distinguished service earned in that first day's operations are so numerous as to testify the great gallantry and ability shown in the actual onset. The D.S.O. was granted to Colonel McNicoll, of Victoria, for his gallantry and skill in leading his battalion into action; and to Colonel White, of the Garrison Artillery, for the skill he displayed in the work of reorganization after the necessary confusion of the landing. Colonel McNicoll was afterwards severely wounded when leading his men forward in the great charge at

Krithia; and at the time of writing lies slowly recovering in a London hospital. Major Brand, of Queensland, carried messages personally under heavy fire on many emergency occasions, and gathered groups of stragglers into a band which, under his command, attacked and disabled three guns. He, and Major Denton, of West Australia, who occupied an important trench with only twenty men, and held it in face of repeated attacks for six days, both got the D.S.O.

Among recipients of the Military Cross was Lieutenant Derham, of Victoria, who was severely wounded in the thigh, but continued to do his duty for five days more in spite of his agony. He returned to Great Britain with five wounds. Captain Richardson, of New South Wales, led his men up the steep path of the cliff into two bayonet charges against bands of Turks five times their number. The men on either side of him were killed, and he had a bullet through his cap. Finally, an expanding bullet struck him on the shoulder, inflicting a terrible wound. Many other officers were rewarded for their grand work on that first day; the instances given are only typical ones that come to hand.

The non-commissioned officers and the rank and file displayed no less bravery and devotion. There was Sergeant Ayling, of Western Australia, who was one of a platoon which got too far forward in an exposed position, and received the command to retire. The officer in charge, Lieutenant Morgan, was severely wounded with shrapnel while this operation was in progress; and Ayling, with three volunteers, returned and drove off the advancing Turks with bayonets, afterwards carrying his wounded officer to safety. Then he reformed his platoon and returned to the attack, holding an exposed position until reinforcements came.

Private Robey, of Queensland, seeing a boat drifting away from the landing-place with a wounded man as its sole occupant, plunged into the water, swam out to the boat under heavy fire, and rescued the comrade from a certain death. Sapper McKenzie, of the Engineers, displayed a similar devotion in carrying a wounded sapper to a departing boat, and pushing it off under heavy fire. He himself was wounded while making for cover. These are only examples among scores of acts of individual bravery displayed on that day of April 25. Some of them have received official recognition; some escaped unrewarded; many of the heroes of that day paid for their gallantry with their lives.

Foremost in heroism on that Sunday were the doctors and stretcher-bearers, of whom the men speak with eyes glowing with enthusiasm. Private Howe, of West Australia, tells how Dr. Stewart, who had wrenched his leg so badly that he had to be invalided, nevertheless picked him up when wounded and carried him on his back under heavy fire for half a mile to a place of safety. Major O'Neill, of New Zealand, has also received the D.S.O. for his bravery and resource in command of bearers.

The Red Cross men were glorious. Most of them worked for thirty-six hours without cessation, and some of them fell down asleep in exposed positions from sheer weariness, as they toiled about the steep rough hillsides at their grand work of mercy. "Two of them saved my life, and I don't even know who they were," said one convalescent Australian. "I was wounded in an exposed trench, and was bleeding quickly to death. My mate wouldn't stand for it; a good chap, but a bit fussy. He signalled back that a man was dying for want of a doctor, and these two chaps came out through the thick of the bullets and carried me off at a sprint. I remember no more until I was on a Hospital ship. They ought not to have come; they risked two good lives to save a doubtful one; and I don't know even who they were and can never thank them." Perhaps those two nameless heroes will see these words one day, and know that their devotion is not forgotten by its grateful object.

Their work was equally as dangerous as that of the fighting soldier, for in those first days of fighting at Gaba Tepe, the Turks made no attempt to respect the Red Cross, though their conduct in this respect improved later on. To advance into the line of fire with a stretcher, under the supposed protection of the Red Cross, was to court a speedy death, and yet there are countless instances of this being done.

One incident, for which a number of witnesses will vouch, shows that this disregard of the Red Cross was part of their training at the hands of their German tutors. A German officer who was lying badly wounded in the firing line attracted the attention of an Australian Red Cross man, who bent over him to render assistance. The return was prompt; the wounded man drew his revolver and shot his benefactor. With a roar of anger, an Australian soldier rushed forward and drove his bayonet time after time through the body of the ungrateful wretch.

The Australian Engineers, who landed about midday on that momentous Sunday, were soon busily at work under the heavy fire directed upon the landing-place. As if by magic, practical paths appeared leading up the cliffside, with sandbag protections; and thus a means of conveying stores and ammunition to the trenches above was at once improvised. The landing-place was improved, and means of getting guns and heavy stores rapidly ashore were contrived with marvellous rapidity. Soon Brighton Beach assumed the appearance of a busy little port, with boats coming and going continually, while shrapnel burst around them and threw up the sand in showers on the beach.

The Australasians completely lost their hearts to the sailormen, with whom they were working here. "I was glad to get out of the blooming boats," said one Australian when recounting his experiences; "but those Jack Tars went to and fro under the shells and bullets as if they never knew of them. You ought to have seen the little middies in charge of the boats; young boys that might have been larking at school. Just boys with round rosy faces, but so keen. When I have a boy I mean to put him in the Australian navy. It makes fine men of them."

The Australasians excited a corresponding admiration from their British sailor friends, not only for the way they fought, but for their whim of bathing under shell fire. Brighton Beach is an ideal place for a swim, barring the small circumstance that several Turkish batteries concealed in the broken ground had the range of the place, and devoted a flattering attention to it. But this did not deter the Australasians, when their time came for a rest, from trying the tonic effect of a plunge in Gallipoli waters.

One man would be stationed on the shore, to give warning, and a score would take to the water together. "Duck," the signalman would cry, as the whining groan of shrapnel shell was heard.

General Birdwood, in charge of the operations at Anzac.

Down would go their heads all together, and up their heels, to disappear under the water just in time to avoid the spray of bullets that tore the smooth surface into foam. Then the sailors, watching the fun through their glasses, would roar with laughter ; and the gasping Australians would show their heads again, to take breath for the next plunge. It sounds reckless, but the practice continued for days, and only one man lost his life through coming up too quickly.

But these amusements were not possible in the few days that followed the first landing. Within twenty-four hours of the appearance of the first warship off Gaba Tepe, the enemy had brought an army of 25,000 men to hold the strongly-prepared positions that commanded the heights above it, and to attempt to drive the Australasians from the precarious footing they had obtained with so much daring. Furious attacks were made all along the line, the object being to prevent the invaders from digging in, and establishing themselves. The 3rd Brigade, which had led the way up the cliffs, and suffered most severely in the initial fighting, had a very hot time of it. They stood firm against repeated bayonet attacks, as did the whole line ; and the work of entrenching went on steadily, in spite of the brave fury with which the Turks repeated their attacks.

The warships gave splendid help, shelling the

main bodies of the defenders wherever they showed on the ridges. The *Queen Elizabeth* was conspicuous in this work, standing off so far to sea that she was hardly discernible, yet landing her gigantic shells with amazing accuracy among the ranks of the Turks. The havoc played by one of these shrapnel shells may be imagined when it is considered that they weigh three-quarters of a ton, and contain 20,000 bullets. Nothing impressed the Australasians more than the hideous din made by the explosion of one of these gigantic shells, and the scar on the hillside that showed after its bursting.

It was under the supporting fire of the warships that the Ninth and Tenth Infantry made a most gallant bayonet charge on the 26th, to drive the Turks from a ridge beyond Pope's Hill, which commanded the whole Australian position, and permitted machine guns to enfilade the landing-place. They advanced in open lines through the scrub, making dashes of a hundred and fifty yards at a swift run, and then dropping to take breath for another charge. Twice they drove the Turks from the position, and were in turn driven back; the third time they stayed there.

The 8th Battalion (Victoria) had to bear the brunt of repeated charges by bodies of Turks who far outnumbered them and came charging with shouts of "Allah! Allah!" The losses sustained by the enemy in these charges were enormous. The 4th (New South Wales) made one dashing bayonet charge that carried them right through the Turkish camp, but beyond they came into an area commanded by machine guns, and got off again, having lost heavily and fought most gallantly.

These are only some of the incidents detailed out of the confusion of the second day's fighting. By the end of that day the Australasians recognized that they were there to stay. A conversation in one of the advanced trenches bears quaintly upon their certainty on this point. One by one the men gazed through a periscope at the prospect commanded from the height they occupied. "Fair country for stock," remarked one, as he yielded his place. "Take a lot of clearing," commented another. The third was a miner. "Here," he said after a long inquisitive look around, "chuck me an entrenching tool; I'm going to try for a prospect."

Yes, they were there to stay right enough; until their duty should call them to fight the cause of right and freedom somewhere else. Already a lamentably large number of them were there to stay until the last trump shall sound the call to them to arise and receive the reward the hereafter holds for brave and noble men, who have laid down their lives that justice and goodness may not perish from the face of the earth. But dead or alive, the Australasians were there to stay.

Already they had made history after a fashion which is testified in a letter written about that time by General Birdwood, who had charge of the whole of the Gaba Tepe operations, to Sir George Reid, the High Commissioner in London for Australia. The General wrote:—

"The capture of the position we at present hold will, I feel sure, go down to history as a magnificent feat of the Australians and New Zealanders. Our one chance of success was to hurl ourselves on the position on a broad front, and just insist on taking it. That is just what we succeeded in doing. We tried our best to effect a surprise by landing at night, though this was necessarily a risky matter, but our one great chance. Our surprise, I fear, was by no means complete, as owing to the moon setting late, our ships were necessarily silhouetted against it as we approached, and we were consequently met with a heavy fire whilst still in the boats. Nothing, however, would stop the men, who just raced ashore, and up and all over this most difficult scrub-covered hill, of which we now hold a portion. In their great zeal, I am sorry to say, some detachments advanced too far, getting right away from the flanks, while the enemy held the centre in strength, and there were, I fear, completely cut off, which made our losses heavy. That, however, could not possibly be avoided, for had commanding officers and brigadiers waited to form

Sir George Reid, High Commissioner for the Australian Commonwealth, 1914-15.

up their commands as they normally would have done, we should probably never have captured the position at all, which great dash alone was able to take."

POPE'S HILL AND GABA TEPE

CHAPTER VI

POPE'S HILL AND GABA TEPE

"I HEARTILY congratulate you on the splendid conduct and bravery displayed by the Australian troops in the operations at the Dardanelles. They have indeed proved themselves worthy sons of the Empire."

When this message, graciously sent by his Majesty King George to the Prime Minister of the Commonwealth of Australia, emerged from the fog of war, there was widespread gratification and pride throughout a continent of 3,000,000 square miles. Nobody knew what the Australians had done, for though more than a week had passed since the Third Brigade made its famous rush up the cliffs at Gaba Tepe, the Censor still nursed the secret of their bravery, lest the waiting nations of the South might communicate it to the powers of darkness in Berlin. The gracious message of the King was the first intimation that Australians were even at the scene of action, and the avidity with which Australasia waited for further details may well be imagined.

Meantime the soldiers of Australasia were fighting hard, and incurring enormous losses to make good their position. Their first important offensive operation, after the actual landing was established, was made against the knoll which now bears the name of Pope's Hill. This position, described by Sir Ian Hamilton as a commanding knoll in front of the centre of the line, was attacked on the night of May 2. Behind it was the head of the deep ravine called Monash Gully, down which the Turks directed a rifle fire so continuous that its outlet on the beach was named Death Valley. The enemy continually sought to extend their advantage to a point which would allow them to direct their fire on the Australians from the other side of the hill also.

The importance of the position can therefore be estimated. It was a sort of no-man's-land, but its possession would give the occupants a great advantage; it certainly would free the Australian lines from a continuous and harassing fire from whole hosts of snipers.

The German officers who directed the Turkish operations had themselves fully seized the value of the post to the invading force, and had posted a number of machine guns with deadly science, covering the whole slope approaching the knoll. When the attack opened on the night of May 2, the attacking force was not long in discovering the arrangements made for its reception. Line after line charged into a perfect hail of bullets from the destructive machine guns, and no less than 800 men were lost before the attackers desisted.

One incident of that terrible day was narrated to the writer by a private of the 15th Battalion who took part in the attack. Early in the morning part of his company was detailed to take a Turkish trench on the slope of the hill. The men crouched in cover about forty yards from the trench waiting a lead. It was given by Lieutenant Kerr, a young South Australian officer, who sprang forward calling on the men to follow. No sooner had he assumed an upright position than he fell dead, with a bullet through his forehead. With a yell of rage the men rushed forward and occupied the trench, bayoneting all the Turks who awaited their coming.

In this operation but few men were lost, though they deeply lamented the death of the brave young officer who had pointed the way to them. But the position soon became a most difficult one to maintain. The Turks appeared in front and to either side of them in overwhelming force, and swept the ground behind them with machine guns, so that none could come to their aid. They maintained a stout defence, until they found to their dismay that their ammunition was running short.

Volunteers were quickly forthcoming to go to the rear for fresh supplies, but they could see them fall one after another, within a few yards of the trench.

They eagerly sought the cartridges still in the belts of the dead and wounded, passing them from hand to hand along the trench, one clip for each man. But this source was soon exhausted, and they were confronted with the fact that they were defenceless and practically cut off. How complete was their isolation they only realized when they saw two machine gun sections of marines attempting to advance up the hill to their assistance. Every man in both sections fell by the side of the guns under the withering fire directed upon them as they climbed upwards.

In this extremity the officer in command, whose name the narrator of the affair could not ascertain, determined to try to reach the communication trench in his immediate rear. He told his men of his resolve, and said he would do all in his power to cover their subsequent retreat, if he succeeded in reaching safety himself. The signal for their retirement would be the hoisting of an entrenching tool in the communication trench.

Having made this arrangement, the officer leaped from the trench and made a dash down the hill. Apparently he took the enemy by surprise, for he reached a safe place without a shot being fired.

Then the shovel was hoisted, and the men prepared to run the gauntlet. One after another eight men bolted from the trench, not one of them going ten yards before being cut off. The ninth was the narrator of this experience

"I knew it was death to stay," he said "and I knew it was almost as surely death to go. I grit my teeth and made a dash for it. I doubled like a hare; I checked and turned and twisted as I ran; the bullets whizzed around me and cut my tunic to rags. Within two yards of safety, and as I was preparing for the last leap into the trench I was struck in the thigh, and the force of the bullet rolled me over among my comrades."

Over two hundred men were lost in the futile attempt to hold that trench alone. For many weeks Pope's Hill remained neutral territory, a menace to the safety of the whole Australasian poition at Gaba Tepe. In the end the Australasians, after capturing and losing it many times, made good their title to the position. Its importance was at once demonstrated by the control it gave them of the high ridge beyond, which they christened Dead Man's Ridge. Before the capture of Pope's Hill the enemy continually shot down Monash Valley, and caused serious casualties every day. Afterwards they were soon cleared from this commanding ridge, and the whole Australasian position was rendered comparatively safe. But this development was deferred for nearly three months after the attack of the second of May.

Another point of vantage is the hill of Gaba Tepe, which is situated on the very seaboard, at the extreme right of the Australasian line. This knoll is only 120 feet high, but the batteries upon it, until they were silenced by the guns of the warships, did an immense amount of damage to landing parties coming and going in the bay. On May 4 an attack was made upon this knoll, but proved unsuccessful, because, to quote the official dispatch of Sir Ian Hamilton, "the barbed wire was something beyond belief." Three months later Gaba Tepe still remained in the hands of the Turks.

The actual losses in these first days of fighting were excessively heavy, and the little force of Australasians, now facing a ring of 25,000 Turks, counted the missing ones ruefully, not only in grief for their dead and wounded comrades, but because the strain placed upon the survivors was by so much the heavier.

The Second Brigade, composed of Victorians led by Colonel McCay, had landed with 4,300 men. After the unsuccessful attack on Gaba Tepe, nine days later, the roll-call showed 2,600 remaining. A week later the same brigade was engaged in a glorious charge at Krithia, and returned with only 1,600

General James McCay, commanding 2nd Brigade, Australian Infantry.

men. In a little over a fortnight that Brigade had lost over 60 per cent. of its effectives, a heavy toll indeed.

The experience of those early days had already taught the adaptable Australasians many new things about bush fighting. They had learned, for instance, how to deal with the snipers who had infested the hillsides ; and in a very short time put an end to them. This was highly necessary, for in the first two or three days' fighting the toll in officers had been intolerable, owing to the efforts of these sharpshooters, whose mission was to pick off the leaders of the men.

The Australian method of stalking them called for a considerable amount of hardihood on the part of those practising it. Two of them would go out after one sniper, having roughly marked down the spot where he lay by the sound of his rifle. They separated as they crawled near him, so that one could approach him from either side. Stealthily they crawled through the olive bush, waiting sometimes for long half hours for the crack of his rifle to assist in locating him. At last the exact thicket that sheltered him would be located ; then, at a given signal, both would rush on him with fixed bayonets. Usually he was alert enough to account for one of them, but the other invariably got him. Those snipers were ready to surrender when caught and held at bay, and the self-control of an Australasian who could spare the enemy who had just shot down his comrade is hard to estimate.

Another new employment was the throwing of bombs, home-made for the greater part. An empty jam tin, with some fuse and explosive, were materials from which the handy bushmen constructed very serviceable bombs, which were employed at that part of the line between Quinn's Post and Courtney's Post, where the trenches approached very closely together.

One team of bomb throwers achieved fame as the Test team, because the sergeant always distributed the ammunition in his own way. He made the distribution a " catching " practice, the bomb forming the cricket ball. The record of no catches missed was well sustained; exactly what might have happened had one been dropped had better be left to the imagination.

During the whole of this time they had heard and seen nothing of their British comrades, who had landed on the southern point of the peninsula of Gallipoli at the same moment as they were scaling the cliffs above Brighton Beach. The German spies who did so much to confuse the initial operations were continually passing word to detached bands to cease firing, as the British, or the French, were immediately in front of them. Little attention was paid to these false statements, except that a vigorous search was made for the originators, and summary justice meted out to them when found. For the Australians were well informed of the movements of the other detachments of the Allied forces.

Between these and the Australasian post at Gaba Tepe towered a range of hills, rising to its highest point at Achi Baba, the Gibraltar of Gallipoli peninsula. The means of communication between the two holdings was limited to the sea, for the Turks were strongly posted, right down to the coast, in the intermediate territory.

By means of the sea, communication was established on May 6 between the two forces; and 4,000 Australasians were detached for the time being to help in the operations of the main body of the Allied armies before the village of Krithia. The men chosen were the Second Brigade of Australians, and the New Zealand infantry. They were taken off on small boats, transferred to trawlers, and carried to the major scene of operations, where they distinguished themselves after a fashion now to be described.

THE CHARGE AT KRITHIA

CHAPTER VII

THE CHARGE AT KRITHIA

THE Australasians were now called upon to take their part in a great concerted attack, made by all the forces commanded by Sir Ian Hamilton on Gallipoli Peninsula. Those familiar with the operations in Gallipoli will remember that, simultaneously with the landing of the Australasians at Gaba Tepe, no less than five landings had been effected by the British and French expeditionary forces further south, on points situated on the extreme southern point of the peninsula.

A great mountain rampart lay between these forces and the Australasians, culminating in the summit of Achi Baba, the hardest nut to crack in the whole peninsula. Loftily situated on the slopes of Achi Baba is the village of Krithia, protected by a maze of Turkish trenches, and a wilderness of barbed wire entanglements. Upon this village an attack was directed from as many points as practicable, and in this attack a large proportion of the Australasian troops participated.

The attack was opened by such a fusillade of

shellfire from the warships of the allied fleet as has seldom been seen or heard. From all quarters they rained shell and shrapnel on the slopes of Krithia, searching the ranges one by one in the attempt to dislodge the defenders from their trenches and hiding-places along the scrubby hillsides and precipitous ravines. The enemies' losses from that shellfire were enormous, but the Turks are admirable defensive fighters, and they clung to their trenches, making the most of the shelters that had been constructed in anticipation of such an attack.

The Australasians had been posted as reserves in this great attack on Krithia, the Australians occupying positions on the left of the Krithia road, in support of a division of the Naval Brigade. On the other side of the road, and in support of the British 88th Brigade, were the New Zealanders. The fighting had begun on May 6, and between then and May 8 some ground had been gained; but the Turks were so strongly entrenched, and counter-attacked so vigorously, that on the morning of the 8th it appeared as though there were some danger of the advantage being again lost.

It was on the evening of May 8 that the long-expected signal to advance was received by the Australasian soldiers. Now they were to prove themselves in the eyes of the world, for they were fighting side by side with men drawn from four continents. Away to their extreme right the French, with their brave Senegalese helping them, had performed prodigies of valour during the preceding days. They were still holding the mile of ground they had gained, hanging on like grim death, and even pushing forward where opportunity permitted.

Nearer to the Australasian posts were Indian troops; Gurkhas, Sikhs and Punjabis; while with them were Britons of all kinds, sailormen and soldiers, regulars, Indian-service men, and a sprinkling of the new Army raised by Lord Kitchener. On the warships in the Gulf of Saros and the Dardanelles, eyes experienced in all the battlefields of modern days were watching them critically. The cannonade from the warships redoubled; the din was appalling, so that the very earth shook with it. It was at this moment that the Australasians were ordered to step into the limelight.

A quarter of a mile in front of the New Zealanders the gallant 88th held a trench. The Maorilanders had to go through that, and forward as far up the slope as a series of rushes with the bayonet would carry them. Before the Australians were the sailormen, situated similarly to the 88th. Past their trench the Australians had to charge, and up the bullet-swept slope towards Krithia. They waited for the signal to advance; it was given by the sudden cessation of the deafening din that was proceeding from the great 15-inch guns of the warships.

With a cry of "Ake! Ake!"—the war cry of the brave old Maori chief Rewi—the New Zealanders swept forward in a solid body over the 400 yards that separated them from the trench held by the 88th. A pause for breath was taken, and then they went on, taking with them many of their English cousins, who wanted to be in it with the bold fellows from the Long White Cloud. Just as they practised evolutions on the sands of Heliopolis, so they performed them now. The solid lines expanded, always advancing without check or pause. Sometimes they doubled, sometimes they walked; but they moved steadily forward all the time, a thin brown line that no human agency could stop. For seven hundred yards more they went on, with bullets raining upon them, and through a veil of constantly exploding shrapnel. Then they could go no farther. But they would not go back; they flung themselves on the ground and dug for shelter.

From the warships that charge was watched by those who were there for no other purpose than to observe and record. The great broken slope up which the charge was made lay like the stage of some huge theatre under the glasses of those who were watching, and with a fascination in which intensest admiration was blended, every move of the soldiers of the South was chronicled. Mr. Ashmead Bartlett was among those who watched that unforget-

The New Zealanders reviewed at Heliopolis.

table charge, and he has placed his impressions on record in the following words :—

"The line entered one Turkish trench with a rush, bayoneted all there, and then passed on into broken ground, shooting and stabbing, men falling amid the terrible fusillade, but not a soul turning back. No sooner had one line charged than another pressed on after it, and then a third. On the right the New Zealanders and the Australians advanced at the same moment, but over much more open ground, which provided little or no cover. They were met by a tornado of bullets and were enfiladed by machine guns from the right.

"The artillery in vain tried to keep down this fire, but the manner in which these Dominion troops went forward will never be forgotten by those who witnessed it. The lines of infantry were enveloped in dust from the patter of countless bullets in the sandy soil and from the hail of shrapnel poured on them, for now the enemy's artillery concentrated furiously on the whole line. The lines advanced steadily as if on parade, sometimes doubling, sometimes walking, and you saw them melt away under this dreadful fusillade only for their lines to be renewed again as the reserves and supports moved forward to replace those who had fallen.

"In spite of all obstacles a considerable advance towards Krithia was made, but at length a point was reached from which it was impossible to proceed farther. Not a man attempted to return to the trenches. They simply lay down where they were and attempted to reply to their concealed enemy, not a man of whom disclosed his position. Only a few hundred yards had been won, it is true, but these Australians and New Zealanders were determined not to budge and proceeded to entrenching themselves where they lay."

The simultaneous charge of the Australians was made with the same steadiness and coolness as was displayed by the New Zealanders. The men were led up to the firing trench occupied by the Naval division by General McCay in person, and he gave them the signal to go forward when they had taken breath after their first quarter of a mile rush. "Now then, on, Australians!" he cried, waving the periscope he carried. And they took up the cry. "Come on, Australians!" was the shout, and there was no need to repeat it.

Through the bursting shrapnel they ran, line after line, always forward, though their ranks were thinning rapidly. They opened out as if on parade, they kept a straight thin line of advance. They raced the New Zealanders on their left and far outdistanced the British and Indians on their right. Then they too dug for shelter, and made good their ground. They were congratulated by their British friends afterwards on the fine show they had made, when one long bushman drawled out, " Why, it was child's play to that first Sunday."

But they had played to a full house and the Australasian charge at Krithia rammed home the reputation they had first won on the steep cliff of Gaba Tepe. On the next day, May 9, the 15th and 16th Battalions of the Fourth Regiment carried three more trenches; and on the following day resisted successfully a series of deadly and persistent attacks. So they won fame in the limelight, and again proved their title to be considered soldiers of the very first rank.

It was after the fighting of these two days that General Sir Ian Hamilton sent to Mr. Andrew Fisher, the Prime Minister of the Australian Commonwealth, a message of which every Australasian should be proud :—" May I, out of a full heart, be permitted to say how gloriously the Australian and New Zealand Contingents have upheld the fine traditions of our race during the struggle still in progress. At first with audacity and dash, since then with sleepless valour and untiring resource, they have already created for their countries an imperishable record of military virtue."

The Australasians holding the position at Gaba Tepe were naturally weakened by the withdrawal of these reinforcements to co-operate in the main attack, and this fact appears to have been known to the enemy. It is at any rate certain that redoubled vigour was displayed in attacking those who remained to hold the Gaba Tepe position, while their comrades were employed elsewhere. All these attacks were successfully repelled, and the defenders, now accustomed to their surroundings, and becoming more inured to actual war conditions, gave even better exhibitions of soldierly qualities than before. That is to say that, while fighting as bravely as ever, they spared themselves more, and reduced the number of avoidable casualties.

But constant and dangerous work had put a great strain upon them, and a rest for many of them was badly needed. At this juncture a very considerable and most welcome reinforcement arrived, and permitted the needed rest to be taken. The reinforcement consisted of the cavalry, who had been left behind in Egypt with their horses. The news that their mates were in the thick of the fighting had not tended to diminish their discontent at being left behind, and on hearing the news from Gaba Tepe, and seeing the first wounded arrive at Egypt, they arose and demanded as one man to be allowed to serve in the trenches as infantry.

Those who know how close and intimate is the tie between the Australasian horseman and his horse will recognize that this volunteering had a special value of its own, coming from the class of man that it did. The offer was gladly accepted, the men doffed their riding-breeches and the rest of their mounted kit, and got into puttees and slacks. They arrived in the nick of time, and any difference between their training and that of the infantry could not be appreciated, as soon as they got into the trenches and to real soldiering work.

The coming of the "light-weights" made a great difference to the men already at Gaba Tepe, whose numbers were sadly depleted; and the men who had left their spurs behind got a welcome all the warmer because they had not waited to be ordered there, but had volunteered. They came in the very nick of time, for the presence of the Australians had become so obnoxious to the German commanders of the Turkish forces that active steps were even then being concerted to get rid of them.

These positions that they hold so strongly midway between the city of Gallipoli and the end of the peninsula, where the bulk of the Expedition to the Dardanelles is operating, are an enormous hindrance to the Turks and their German masters. A large body of troops must always be kept on the spot to prevent the Australasians from cutting communications between the main defending force and the depots whence they draw their stores and reinforcements. Not only that; the actual progress of reinforcements is hampered by the operations of these tireless Colonials, who are constantly harassing the warrior natives of the soil.

Therefore General Liman von Sanders, in his wisdom, decided that the Australasians must be driven into the sea; and at the time of the arrival of the reinforcements drawn from the Australasian Light Horse, was gathering a strong army, which he soon afterwards directed in a general frontal attack upon the Australasian positions.

But before that attack was delivered, the Australian army suffered an irreparable loss in the person of its brave and skilful General, General Bridges. This gallant soldier had been in the thick of the fighting throughout the whole of the operations that began with the landing of April 25. Wherever he went he set an example of cool courage that acted as a tonic to the men, who trusted and loved him dearly. At first he disdained to take the ordinary precautions that were dictated by the conditions under which he was directing operations, and with a grim carelessness walked about under shrapnel fire, without making any attempt to seek cover.

The warnings of his staff, and his early conviction that it was not necessary to set so uncompromising an example of personal courage to men so consistently brave as those under his command, caused him later to adopt a more prudent attitude; and

General Bridges, who commanded the 1st Expeditionary Force from Australia. Died from a wound inflicted by a sniper in the Valley of Death on May 10,

on the day when he sustained his fatal wound he showed more than his customary care for himself. He set out upon an inspection of a firing line, and for once he consented to run through the more exposed parts of his round.

A description has already been given of the deep ravine that runs down to the sea on the right of Pope's Hill. When he came to the path that crosses this gully, he was warned by the dressers at the ambulance station that the bullets were flying very thickly down the gully. "You had better run across here, sir," said one of them. He took the advice and reached another shelter. There he stood for a time, and then remarking ruefully, "Well, I suppose I must run for it again," he made a dash for the next cover. Before he reached it a bullet struck him in the thigh, severing an important artery. He would have rapidly bled to death but for prompt assistance. Stricken as he was, his first thought was for others; he did not wish any one to expose himself in helping to carry him down to the sea-front.

He was carried there, however, and transferred to the hospital ship with every possible care. In spite of all attention and skill, he never rallied; and died at sea on his way to Egypt. Australia mourns him as a gallant and considerate leader, a man whose memory will be ever revered in the Southern Continent. His command was temporarily assumed by Brigadier-General Walker, who acted in that capacity until the arrival from Australia of Colonel Legge, who was appointed to succeed General Bridges.

General Legge, who succeeded General Bridges.

THE BATTLE OF QUINN'S POST

CHAPTER VIII

THE BATTLE OF QUINN'S POST

CAPTAIN VON MUELLER boasted that he would sink the Australian cruiser *Sydney*. He lost his ship, and was carried a captive by the Australians to a British prison camp. General Liman von Sanders declared he would drive the Australasians off the face of Gallipoli Peninsula into the sea. The result of his attempt was a slaughter of Turks that has not been equalled in the Dardanelles fighting, and the return of so many wounded to Constantinople that a panic was created in the Turkish capital. If any boasting is to be done, the proper time is after the event.

The preparations made by Sanders Pasha for his great attack upon the Australasians were long and elaborate. For days beforehand he was busy in organizing the transport of great stores of ammunition to the neighbourhood of Maidos, a town on the neck of the peninsula, opposite Gaba Tepe. Five fresh regiments were brought from Constantinople to stiffen the attacking force; they afterwards proved to have been chosen from the very *élite* of the Turkish army. He detached in addition heavy reinforcements from the main body of defenders, who were holding back the Allies at Achi Baba. He had determined to do the thing very thoroughly.

His attack was launched on May 18, and he himself assumed personal charge of the operations. Shortly before midnight on May 18 he began to expend his huge store of shell after the approved German fashion. All the batteries concealed in the hills around set up a hideous din, swollen by the roar of the machine guns, and the cracking of countless rifles. In that shelling, 12-inch guns, 9-inch guns, and huge howitzers were employed, as well as artillery of smaller calibre. Naturally every Australasian was on the look out; and word was sent to every post to be prepared for the frontal attack it was assumed would follow. The assumption was a correct one; for soon countless Turks poured over the ridges and made for the centre of the Australasian line.

It has already been explained that this line is a rough semicircle, the left, or Northern wing being situated on high ground above Fisherman's Hut. Here is a ridge facing North-East, named Walker's Ridge after Brigadier-General Walker, and to the right of that is Pope's Hill. These spots are North of the great central gully or valley, which was

General Monash, Commander of the 4th Brigade, Australian Infantry.

at first known as Death Gully by the Australian
soldiers, but is now called Monash Gully, after
General Monash, commander of the 4th Brigade.
Immediately to the right of the Gully is Dead
Man's Ridge, and the point where the line takes
a sharp turn to the South is known as the Bloody
Angle.

The Turkish lines, which are some 250 yards
distant at the extreme left of the position, continue to get closer to those of the Australasians
until here they approach very closely. At Quinn's
Post, named after a gallant Major from Queensland
who fell fighting bravely at the spot, the lines are
only twenty yards apart. The gap widens going
South to Courtney's Post, and continues to do so
through the other main positions at McLaurin
Hill, down to Point Rosenthal, which faces Gaba
Tepe itself on the extreme right wing.

Quinn's Post, at the extreme curve of the Australasian semicircle, came in for the hottest attack
of all. In this part of the line were stationed the
Fourth Infantry Brigade, which comprised the
bulk of the Second Australian Contingent, and is
commanded by General Monash. Of this 4th
Brigade more will soon be told, but it suffices to
say that their steadiness and fighting qualities were
put to the supreme test on this early morning of
May 19. The trenches here faced the ridge called
Dead Man's Ridge, and over this ridge the Turks

pushed one another to the attack. Their advance was covered by a continuation of the heavy bombardment of the trenches from Hill 700, and from the top of the ridge where guns, heavy, light and machine, had been concentrated.

This fire, added to the bullets from thousands of rifles, kept all Australasian heads down. Bravely the Turks dashed through the scrub, taking all the cover it afforded, and regardless of the field guns and howitzers of the Australians, which were concentrated on them with deadly effect. Many of them got right up to the edge of the trenches, and were shot down at point-blank range. Still they crept out of their cover, massing in every thicket, and advancing under pressure of those behind.

The first light of early morning revealed to the waiting Australians a dense mass of the enemy, exposed and within easy range. Then the rifles of the best shots in the world—for there are at least no superiors to them anywhere—rang out, and as fast as each man could pull the trigger, the Turk fell under that deadly fusillade. Still they poured over the ridges, their officers driving them on from behind with loaded revolvers, and still the discriminate slaughter went on.

It was discriminate slaughter, for each Australian, before he fired, marked his man and made sure of him. It was no time for sentimental considerations of mercy; and besides, the Australians

Australian Field Artillery in Action.

were fierce with the anger of men who had been sniped for three weeks, without too many chances of getting their own back. They had charged against positions held as their own now was, and had seen their bravest and best fall by hundreds as they drove on in the face of shrapnel and machine-gun fire. Now it was their turn, and they fired until the barrels of their rifles got too hot to be touched. "It was like killing rabbits with a stick," said one man, who was in the hottest part of the fray.

All along the line from Quinn's Post to Courtney's the dead were piled in heaps ; and still they came on. Some of them died grasping the barbed wire protections in front of the trenches, others fell dead into the very trenches themselves, only stopped by a bullet met on the parapet. They had the support of all the guns Sanders Pasha had been able to muster, and all his huge store of ammunition was expended in trying to drive those Australians into the sea. But not a man budged from his post.

From daylight till ten o'clock that morning the bombardment and the frontal attack were continued ; then the Turks would have no more of it. Sullenly they fell back, and as they did so shrapnel completed the disorganization which had now begun. Soon after ten they turned and ran for their trenches, and there they sheltered for hours while the heavy cannonade continued. In the middle of the afternoon their officers made another attempt to drive them forward, but it was a half-hearted response that was elicited. Once more they faced that deadly accurate rifle fire of the men from the South, and before it they crumpled up and fled again for shelter. All night they kept up an incessant fire from their trenches, but in the morning it died away into nothingness. General Liman von Sanders had made a mistake, and the most expensive mistake yet made on the peninsula of Gallipoli. Such was the end to his boasting.

Not a Turk had entered an Australian trench except dead Turks, not a yard of ground had been gained in any direction. And from Quinn's Post all along the line to Courtenay's, the ground was piled with the dead and dying. "Eight acres of dead bodies," estimated one literal bushman, after a close scrutiny of the field of battle through a periscope. Another essayed to count the bodies in sight from his trench, and stopped at an estimate of 4,000. At least 30,000 Turks took part in that frontal attack, and on a conservative estimate, one-third of them were put out of action. The wounded were sent back to Constantinople literally by thousands, and the sight of them spread panic and dismay far and wide through that city.

Mr. Ashmead Bartlett, who went over the lines on the following day, presents a grim picture of the slaughter wrought by the straight-shooting Australians.

"The ground presents an extraordinary sight when viewed through the trench periscopes. Two hundred yards away, and even closer in places, are the Turkish trenches, and between them and our lines the dead lie in hundreds. There are groups of twenty or thirty massed together, as if for mutual protection, some lying on their faces, some killed in the act of firing; others hung up in the barbed wire. In one place a small group actually reached our parapet, and now lie dead on it, shot at point-blank range or bayoneted. Hundreds of others lie just outside their own trenches, where they were caught by rifles and shrapnel when trying to regain them. Hundreds of wounded must have perished between the lines, for it was only on the 21st that the enemy made overtures for an armistice for burying the dead; but up to the present this has not been granted owing to the suspicious number of troops in his front trenches.

"In places the Turks made four or five separate efforts to charge home, using hand-grenades, but they all failed dismally."

"Ever alert," writes one who took part in the slaughter, "the Colonials were ready to meet the strain when it came. The sight of seemingly endless masses of the enemy advancing upon them might well have shaken the nerve of the already severely-tried troops. Our machine guns and artillery mowed down the attackers in hundreds, but still the advancing wall swept on. On, still! Would the ranks never waste in strength? Not till the wave was at point-blank range from the nimble trigger-fingers did it break and spend itself amongst our barbed-wire entanglements. Turks were shot in the act of jumping into our trenches. Corpses lay with their heads and arms hanging over our parapets. Our fire gradually dominated the ground in front. Those who turned to fly were mowed down before they could go a dozen yards. The Germans sent their supports forward in droves. It was sickening to behold the slaughter our fire made amongst the massed battalions as they issued from concealment into open spaces.

"These unfortunate Turks scrambled along towards us over piles of dead bodies. In an instant a company would be enveloped in the smoke of a shrapnel salvo. When the smoke cleared that company would be stretched or writhing on the ground, with another company approaching and ready to share its predecessor's fate."

The Australasians did not lose one man for every twenty they put out of action. Coolly and methodically they took the chance sent them by Sanders Pasha, and every bullet was sent home in memory of the brave comrades they had lost,

IN THE GREAT WAR 125

and the grand general who was even then breathing his last. They had previously displayed bravery, hardihood, and resource beyond imagination; the qualities shown at the battle of Quinn's Post were steadiness, accurate shooting, and a reasoned discipline that would have done the utmost credit to the most seasoned veterans of the British regular army.

Two days later the Turks craved an armistice to bury their thousands of slain. Too great indulgence could not be given them in the performance of their gruesome task, for under the tuition of their German masters they are apt to employ such breathing spaces for purposes to which they ought not to be devoted. The requests for armistices became very frequent after that slaughter of May 19, but the Australasians knew just how to deal with them.

And so the Australasians got their own back with enormous interest. After being sent forward over open country against big fields of barbed wire, with enfilading machine guns hidden at every turn, it was a sheer luxury to lie in the trenches and let the other fellow do a bit of self-immolation. They knew, too, that they had struck a deadly blow at German prestige with the Turk. General Birdwood told them so when he inspected their defences, after the fight was over.

A THORN IN THE FLESH

CHAPTER IX

A THORN IN THE FLESH

THE failure of the attempt to drive the Australasians into the sea was followed by two months of desultory fighting that resembled nothing so much as the deadlock between the Allies and the Germans in the North of France. The operations, of course, were on a scale infinitely smaller, and the Australasians held the advantage of occupying the position of invaders. They were, indeed, a thorn in the flesh of the Turkish army, for they held a position with infinite possibilities.

The object of the whole land expedition in Gallipoli is to obtain command of that part of the straits of the Dardanelles known as the Narrows, where Europe and Asia are only separated by a mile of sea water. Here are the strongest of the forts built by the Turks to protect the passage of the Dardanelles. Before this narrow passage lies a minefield so thick that it defied the attempt of the fleet of the Allied Powers to force a passage through the Dardanelles to Constantinople. An attempt to dredge the minefield with trawlers was defeated by hidden batteries on the very heights for which the Australasians are fighting, and also by the guns of the forts at the Narrows.

At the southern point of the peninsula the main force of the Allies is attempting to cut a way through to a tableland known as the Plateau of Kilid Bahr, which dominates the European coast of the Dardanelles from the entrance as far as the Narrows themselves. The spot occupied by the Australasians on the Gulf of Saros is opposite the town of Maidos on the straits, and therefore above the Narrows. This much must be grasped in order to understand the possibilities arising from the existence of an Australasian force in that spot, and the precautions forced upon the Turks because they remain there.

The main body of the Turkish army is concerned with the defence of the fort of Achi Baba and all the strong positions centring in that height. All supplies for this defence force must come from the base at Constantinople, by sea to Gallipoli, and thence by road through Maidos, the town threatened by the Australasians. Moreover, all reinforcements must pass by the same way; and the heavy losses inflicted upon the Turks by the Allied forces in Gallipoli have necessitated many reinforcements.

Therefore the presence of the Australasians around the hill of Sari Bair, even while they re-

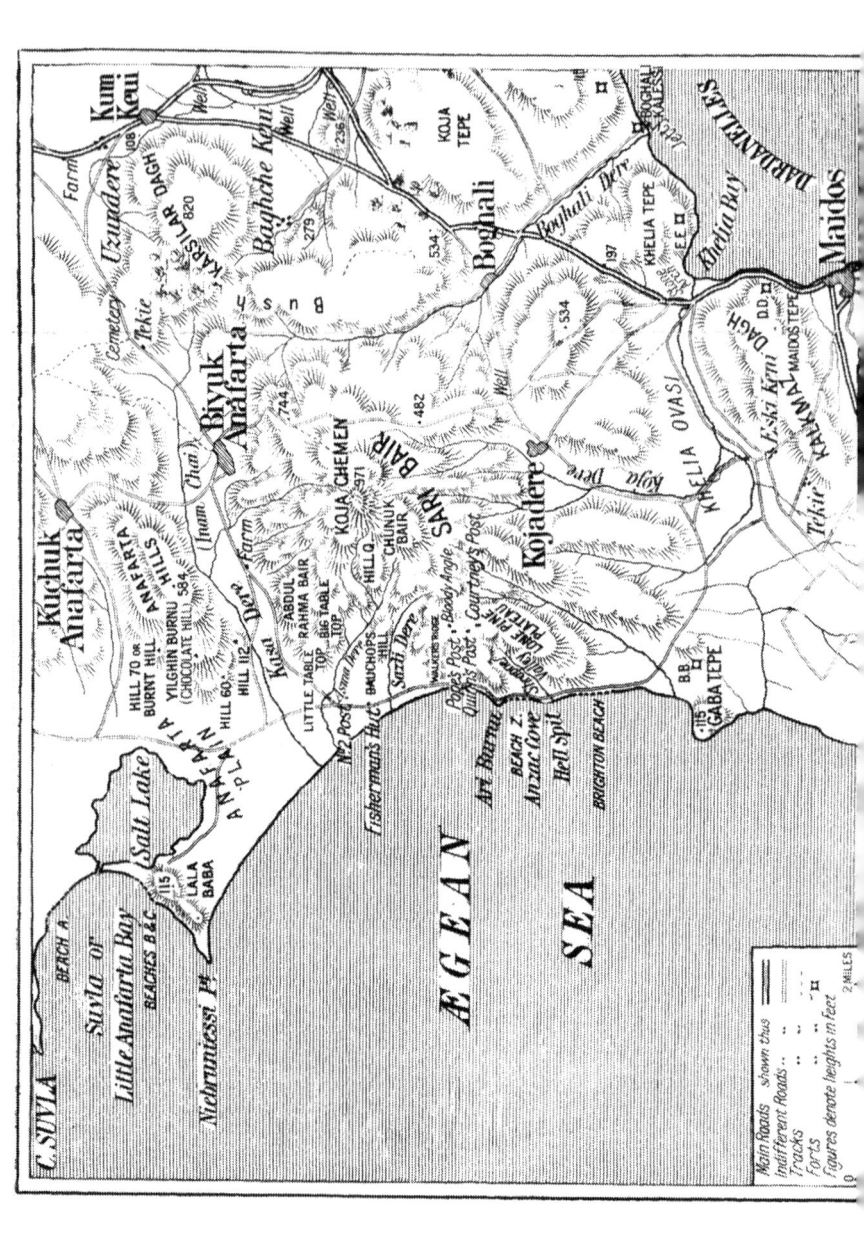

mained passive, forced the Turks to maintain a force of from 25,000 to 30,000 men at this point, merely to keep them in check. For two months the slightest sign of any diminution of that force was the signal for a demonstration by the Australasians, which at least had the effect of bringing the Turks back to the trenches they are so anxious to vacate.

Eventually the Australasians were so strengthened that they were able to resume the offensive which they had dropped in the early days of May, recognizing that their numbers were not great enough to permit of such measures. But during the latter part of May, and through the months of June and July, they were forced to mark time steadily, and jealously to conserve the little patch of ground they had won with such incredible audacity on the cliffs of Sari Bair. The extent of that holding may be gauged when it is stated that the beachline was a little over two miles long, and that the furthest point inland of the Australasian line was not more than a mile from the sea, as a crow flies. Thus the Australasians were clinging on to a little more than two square mile of the Gallipoli peninsula; and for two months never lost an inch of it, but steadily consolidated their holding.

Mining and sapping went on all day and all night, and the Turks have proved themselves masters at this underground warfare. The Australasians replied in kind, and the outcome of some of these adventures was lively hand-to-hand fighting. On May 29 the Turks got a sap close up to the Australasian line, and occupied two shell craters within four yards of the trenches. They soon turned them into bombproof shelters, and were established there before they were discovered.

Three men of the 15th Battalion of the Australasian Force, Sergeant Kidd, and privates Stronach and Birch, have written the following account of what followed, and placed it at the disposal of the writer. All three men were wounded in the fighting of that May 29. Their account runs:

"Everything was quiet on the morning of May 29. At the hour of 3 a.m. a few rifles rang out from time to time, but for Quinn's Post this was comparative silence. Suddenly a bright glare shot skywards, followed by intense darkness, and a deep reverberating roar—the Turks had blown our trenches up. Almost simultaneously with the sound of the explosion an uproar of rifle and machine gun fire burst from the enemy's trenches, and was answered from ours, making a din in which it was impossible to hear an order, unless shouted in one's very ear.

"We stood to arms and in five minutes we rushed up the hill in the faintly gathering dawn. The enemy's artillery had the range, and their shells burst continuously overhead, lighting up the rugged sides of the great ravine like a terrific thunder-storm. The detonation of the guns, fired incessantly, reverberated through the hills and gullies and increased the likeness to some titanic tempest, while the sight of the ever-increasing stream of wounded we met coming down hill, all covered with blood and maimed and crippled, added to the terror of the moment.

"When we reached the hill-top we found the worst had happened: the Turks had got possession of three lines of trenches. The duty of turning them out fell to our battalion, the Fighting Fifteenth. As the faint light broadened to day we lined up and awaited the word to charge. If any one says that at such a moment he felt no anxiety or terror, let him be branded as a liar and empty braggart. No man should face death without some tremor, let alone the hail of bombs which the victorious Turks threw over from the conquered trenches, and which seem to hold a terror in themselves that is even worse than death.

"Yet it was through this screen of horror that we had to dash, and by sheer force drive the enemy out of their newly-acquired position. Clear above all other noises shrilled a whistle; and with a yell each man dashed forward. There was a confused glimpse of men falling, and of others staggering back through the smoke, all streaming with blood and with limbs shattered by the hideous bombs. But in thirty seconds the communication trench was clear.

"From the support trench, which was full of Turks, there poured a hail of bullets and grenades, causing us to reel and fall back for a breathing space. Then our own bomb throwers stepped forward and hurled bombs into the trench, whence fragments of shattered humanity leaped up into the air. The desperate men sprang from the trench and bravely charged, but ten yards was as far as they got; under our deadly rifle and machine gun fire they went down like wheat before the scythe.

"We counter-charged in the next moment and scores of our fellows went over the parapet into the trench, where the stabbing blows of the bayonet could be heard for a good three minutes. Then the firing line was ours again.

"But the support trench in the centre still held out. Owing to the bombproof shelter there was no possible way of shifting the stubborn defenders. Bravely they fought for their footing but the use of bombs convinced them of the hopelessness of the position they occupied. Finally they surrendered; and came out covered with blood and dust, eighteen limping heathen heroes. We hope we showed them due respect, the respect we felt for their brave fight.

"Then came the task of clearing the trench of the dead, a gruesome work. Poor shattered fragments of humanity, without any likeness to the human form remaining had to be gathered up in sandbags and carried away. No words can paint the hideous thoroughness with which the grenades do their devilish work. So ended the fight of May 29."

The craters were also taken by a body of Light Horse who, after throwing a large number of bombs into the craters, boldly leaped in, with their bayonets fixed. They cleared the holes of Turks, though all of the attacking force were wounded but two, and the greater part of them were isolated in the craters for a night. But they held the craters until relief could be sent them.

This necessitated some brisk work by an Australian machine-gun section, in the course of which one young gunner distinguished himself by bravery and devotion of the highest order. He was engaged against two Turkish machine guns, and continued to work his own gun, though they were cutting away his parapet of sandbags, and must eventually expose him to a stream of bullets. The maintenance of his fire was of the utmost importance, since it covered a series of operations by a considerable force of men. At last he fell back wounded, but not until he had saved the situation by his devoted bravery.

With a little experience, the Australasians became in their turn first-class sappers.

"I am a voluntary sapper now," writes one of them, "digging a tunnel to some new trenches we have dug just behind a ridge about 100 yards in front of the Turks' trenches. We went out one night to dig them in moonlight, and they opened a pretty brisk fire for a bit, but we were practically safe behind the ridge; all the same, we were ready for them. Three of the evening party got hit, but most of the damage was done by fellows bumping their picks into one another, tearing the seats of their trousers out, etc. Some of our saps go through dead Turks buried during the armistice before we came. We wash ourselves and clothes in the sea, as fresh water is too scarce for anything but drinking purposes just yet."

A diversion from this trench warfare was occasioned on June 28 by an attempt on the part of the Turks to withdraw part of their forces for use in the more southerly part of the peninsula. The Australasians replied with a strong attack. It opened in the regular way by the ships bombarding the hillsides. Then the 2nd Light Horse and the 3rd Infantry advanced 700 yards, and gave the Turks something to think about. This produced a counter-attack, which was repulsed by the Australasians with heavy loss to the enemy. Then, having fulfilled their mission, the Australasians retired in good order within their lines.

They are now thoroughly familiar with the strange rough country of Gallipoli, of which one of them writes:—

"The world seems to have been built up on end, and the high cliffs are accessible only by the spurs and valleys. The place is very different now— roads have been cut and built, and steep as they are, mules can reach the top fairly easily. It is very exasperating to look out on the peaceful flat country just a few miles away with peaceful homesteads in places. Our chief pastime in life is smashing Turkish periscopes, of which they don't possess very many. It is good target practice, and helps to prevent them from being too perky. At present we are just marking time, and things are rather quiet."

But toward the end of July the period of marking time ended, and very important developments took place at Sari Bair. While they had been waiting, reinforcements had been pouring over to Egypt from Australia and New Zealand, and a force five times as great as the original landing party was gathered together. More men were landed at Sari Bair, and a fresh landing was also effected at a point a little further north, marked on the map as Ari Burnu. While this landing was being effected an attack in force was delivered by the Australasians at the extreme right of the line, where they won an important ridge known as Tasmania Ridge.

The success of this operation was due in part to the withdrawal of the Turks to resist the landing at Ari Burnu. Thus the Australasians gained an important advantage. In the same operation the Turks proved unequal to the task of preventing the landing, or the occupation of a high point of the Sari Bair mountain ridge known as Chunuk Bair.

Between the first and the twelfth of August the Australasians pushed their advantage so keenly that they trebled the area of land held by them in Gallipoli, gaining some positions of the utmost importance to the whole scheme of operations in the peninsula. Their strength had been so increased that the original number of 12,000 landed on April 25 had been swollen to 130,000 by the beginning of August. Allowing for all casualties, this would leave them an effective fighting force of quite 100,000 men at Sari Bair, a very formidable army indeed, composed as it is, of audacious and enterprising soldiers.

The landing of so great a force on that position demonstrated conclusively what had long been in the minds of most close students of the fighting at the Dardanelles. This was that the key to the whole situation in the Dardanelles was held by the Australasian Forces. That conclusion was emphasized by Colonel St. Clair Cameron, General Birdwood's adviser, who reported that the capture of the Narrows would be the inevitable result of a proper strengthening of the forces at Sari Bair. The main points of his report were published in the Australasian papers early in June and did much to stimulate the wonderful recruiting which took place in Australia and New Zealand in the middle of the year.

FILLING THE GAPS

CHAPTER X

FILLING THE GAPS

FROM Blackboy to Mena, from Mena to where
They drew the first blood with the bayonet,
They hoisted the heathen foe out of his lair
Who'd the Germanized courage to stay in it.
From Suez they scattered the truculent Turk,
To far Teheran and to Tripoli;
And at last they beheld British Jackies at work
On the gun-bristled hills of Gallipoli:
  On the gun-bristled hills of Gallipoli,
A minute of wading in bullet-splashed waves,
The Cooees of Motherland thrilling 'em.
But those minutes cut holes in that brown line of braves
And—What about filling 'em ?

So wrote one of Australia's bards when the first news of the battle of Brighton Beach reached the Commonwealth. The practical patriotism of Australia at once grasped the fact that there must be wide gaps in the ranks, and that the best reward the Commonwealth could make to those who had upheld the honour of Australasia so nobly was to support them with all the additional men and money required for the completion of the task so nobly begun.

But Australia had no notion how wide were the gaps torn in the ranks of her brave sons during the fighting that took place in those first fierce days at Gaba Tepe. From the date of landing to the end of June the losses among the Australasians totalled nearly 14,000 men, or an average of 200 men for each day during the nine weeks of the Australasian occupation of Gallipoli. It has already been stated that the original Expeditionary Force from Australasia totalled 28,000 men in all; but even before they had left Southern waters, arrangements for further contingents were well advanced. As a matter of fact, the second contingent, which was 10,000 strong, had arrived in Egypt in time to take part in the training at Mena, and was part of the landing force of April. With the New Zealanders the infantry of this contingent served under General Sir A. J. Godley as the 4th Brigade, and reference has already been made to their gallant defence of the central position at the battle of Quinn's Post, where Sanders Pasha led the Turks to an irretrievable disaster.

Their General expressed his personal opinion of the services of the gallant 4th at Anzac on June 2, when he gathered the men together and delivered to them the following inspiriting address :—

" Colonel Monash, officers, non-commissioned officers and men of the Fourth Australian Infantry

General Sir A. J. Godley commanding the New Zealanders and the 4th Brigade, Australian Infantry.

Brigade :—I have come here to-day to tell you all with what great pride and satisfaction I have watched your performances for the past five weeks, and to tell you also that not only your comrades in this division, but also those of the whole Australasian Army Corps, have looked on with the greatest admiration at your gallant doings, from the moment that you landed in the Gallipoli Peninsula. You have been for five weeks continuously in the front trenches, fighting particularly hard the whole of that time. Never have troops been subjected to such heavy shell and rifle fire, not to speak of bombs and hand grenades; you have lived and fought in a din and turmoil which would have sorely tried most men. You began your fighting immediately on landing, pitchforked, I might say, into the middle of the battle, with the whole brigade scattered in small fragments in different parts of the firing line, as the several units landed. You were in the firing line continuously for seven days with nothing but what you carried on you. It took days of hard work for the brigadier and his staff to collect the battalions together and to consolidate the section of defence allotted to this brigade. During this time many deeds of heroism, many acts of gallantry were performed, which will remain unknown and will go unrewarded, and many of your comrades were killed and wounded. Again, on May 2 and 3, this brigade undertook a sortie from its lines which was very far-reaching in its results, and which shattered the enemy's plans for a combined assault most effectually. Again, on May 9, this brigade made another highly successful sortie, and only a few days ago, during the greater part of May 18 and 19, you bore the brunt of the very severe Turkish attack by which the enemy hoped to drive this army corps into the sea.

"Yours is a fine record, and one of which you yourselves, and the whole of the people of Australia, have the fullest reason to be proud. You have made, and are making, the military history of Australia—a history equal to that of any other brigade or body of troops in the Empire, or in the world—and you have performed deeds, and achieved successes, of which the Commonwealth will surely be proud. Pope's Hill position is named after the gallant commander of the 16th Battalion, which held it so long against such odds; Courtney's Post will for ever be associated with the 14th Battalion, which has defended it against all attacks for the whole period; the most difficult post of all—Quinn's Post, named after Major Quinn, who bravely died at this post in the service of his country, and who, I am sure, would have preferred no more glorious death—this post will be for ever associated with the name of Lieut. Colonel Cannon, and the 15th Battalion. Nor will be forgotten the gallant behaviour of the 13th Battalion, under Lieut.-Colonel Burnage, who, among many other fine performances, held on for a night and a day in a difficult advanced position, which they had stormed, and from which they did not withdraw until ordered to do so in view of the subsequent course of the operations.

"Among so many whose names are worthy of record and distinction, it has been very hard to single out individuals, but as commander of this division, I have had the honour of sending on the names of some twenty officers and men, from that of your brigadier downwards, for special and honourable mention in despatches for most meritorious service and conspicuous gallantry.

"It has pleased his Majesty the King to confer upon this brigade eleven honours, comprising two Distinguished Service Orders, two Military Crosses, and seven Distinguished Conduct medals. These rewards, earned between the landing of the brigade on April 25 and May 5, are surely a rare and enviable distinction.

"On behalf of the Imperial Government, because of the great services you have rendered to the glory of the Empire—greater services than you probably yourselves realize—I thank you, Colonel Monash, your staff, your commanding officers, and all your personnel from the highest to the lowest, for the work you have done during the past five weeks."

This second contingent, which distinguished itself so remarkably from the time of its landing, was followed by yet a third, also of 10,000 men, led by Colonels Spencer Browne, C.B., V.D.; W. Holmes, D.S.O. V.D.; and Linton. They were of physique equal in every respect to their forerunners, and may be trusted to render an equally good account of themselves.

These supplementary contingents are to be regarded as additions to the first Expeditionary force, for the Australian method of filling the gaps is to send monthly reinforcements, sufficient to replace all men lost in battle. The original estimate was for 3,000 a month, but when the Australian Government grasped the serious nature of the operations in which their men were engaged, and the extent of the casualty lists, they increased this number to 4,000 monthly. These steps were taken before the full accounts of the Gallipoli fighting had reached Australia; they provided merely for what was thought a serious operation bearing a prospect of success at no remote date in the future.

But the full grandeur of Australian patriotism was only to be realized when it was gathered that the whole Turkish army was mustered in defence of the Straits of the Dardanelles, and that Australasia was called upon to bear a very considerable share of a separate war, waged against the full strength of a desperate warrior nation. Then Australasia became one vast recruiting ground; and military enthusiasm reached a pitch which has not yet been realized in the Mother Country.

It would be a salutary lesson to that section of the London Press which persists in a sour pessimistic view of the whole of the Dardanelles adventure to be made to reprint a few columns of the sane but ardent patriotism with which the Australians were spurred by their worthy Press to shoulder the load which has been apportioned to them. There were none of those hints of possible failure which have so appalled the unsophisticated Briton during the summer months of 1915. A nation of 5,000,000 people that prepares to put 250,000 men down on the spot, and back them with its last shilling, cherishes no such unworthy doubts. A more splendid answer to croakers than that given by Australasia could hardly have been devised.

For the Commonwealth set itself seriously to put an army of a quarter of a million men in the field. Only cabled accounts of that wave of recruiting energy, which converted Australia into a great armed camp, have yet reached this country. But they make the heart swell with pride at the indomitable courage with which the Southern Nations are preparing to tackle the problem of the Gallipoli Peninsula.

The cost was laid before Parliament and, after consideration, approved without question. An expenditure of £40,000,000 was faced without a murmur. "In three months' time," said a responsible minister, "Australia would be paying more per head for the war than the people in England." The statement was received with cheers. The suggestion of a war tax met with no opposition in the House of Parliament; nor from the mass of the Australian people. The money is to be found without any grumbling.

As for the men, they sprang to the call. The State of Victoria showed the way with a great recruiting campaign, with the avowed object of getting a thousand men per day. At the end of a fortnight the record was 18,970 applications, of which 13,810 were accepted. On the same scale of recruiting, the United Kingdom would yield nearly 500,000 soldiers in a fortnight. The figures, in proportion to population, seem almost incredible, but they are accurate.

The Mother State of New South Wales followed with a similar campaign. One city of less than 100,000 people—the city of Newcastle—provided 363 applicants in one day. On the same lines recruiting was organized all over Australia; as these words are written it is going on with such enthusiasm that there can be no doubt of the result. These farmers and stock-raisers are facing

A New South Wales Battalion, ready for the Front.

the best season the country has ever been promised, they leave their bumper harvest to ripen and be gathered by the women and boys; it is for them to see this business through "on the gun-bristled hills of Gallipoli."

The spirit of Australia can best be gauged by reading an extract from a letter written to the Australian wounded by a young lady who is a teacher at the High School in Ballarat, and which was cabled all over the world, since it echoes truly the pride of Australia in its heroes, and the determination of the Commonwealth that all shall be worthy of their devotion and grand patriotism. The letter was received at the hospital at Malta, and runs as follows :—

"*May* 12.

"DEAR AUSTRALIAN BOYS,—Every Australian woman's heart this week is thrilling with pride, with exultation, and while her eyes fill with tears she springs up as I did when the story in Saturday's *Argus* was finished and says, 'Thank God, I am an Australian.' Boys, you have honoured our land; you, the novices, the untrained, the untaught in war's grim school, have done the deeds of veterans. Oh, how we honour you; how we glory in your matchless bravery, in your yet more wonderful fortitude, which the war correspondent says was shown so marvellously as your boatloads of wounded cheered and waved amid their pain as you were rowed back to the vessels!

"What gave you the courage for that heroic dash to the ridge, boys? British grit, Australians' nerve and determination to do or die, a bit of the primeval man's love of a big fight against heavy odds. God's help, too, surely.

"Dear boys, I'm sure you will feel a little rewarded for your deeds of prowess if you know how the whole Commonwealth, nay, the whole Empire, is stirred by them. Every Sunday now we are singing the following lines after 'God save the King' in church and Sunday school. They appeared in the *Argus Extraordinary* with the first Honour Roll in it:

> God save our splendid men!
> Send them safe home again!
> Keep them victorious,
> Patient and chivalrous,
> They are so dear to us:
> God save our men.

"What can I say further? With God the ultimate issue rests. Good-night, boys. God have you living or dying in His keeping. If any one of you would like to send me a pencilled note or card I'll answer it to him by return.—Your countrywoman,

"JEANIE DOBSON."

That Australian purses were opened with Australian hearts is proved by the remarkable total of gifts in money and kind made by Australia to various funds on behalf of sufferers by the war. In the first ten months the Commonwealth contributed in cash the sum of £2,329,259 to the various funds arising out of the war, apart from immense gifts in kind, the value of which is not estimatable. The State contributions are totalled as follows :—New South Wales, £980,889 ; Victoria, £850,000 ; Queensland, £200,825 ; South Australia, £127,540 ; Tasmania, £36,750 ; and Western Australia, £133,255. Total, £2,329,259.

The Australian care for the wounded is the subject of a testimony from Sir Frederick Treves, which may be included here to show the appreciation with which this care has been met by the most eminent surgeon in the Empire :—

"The generosity with which Australia has provided motor ambulances for the whole country, and Red Cross stores for every one, British or French, who has been in want of the same, is beyond all words. I only hope that the people of Australia will come to know of the admirable manner in which their wounded have been cared for, and of the noble and generous work which that great colony has done under the banner of the Red Cross."

New Zealand is no whit behind Australia ; indeed, in proportion to population, the Dominion supplied more men during the first ten months of the war than even the Commonwealth. The troops actually sent on active service by this community of a little more than a million people were :—

First Samoan Force	2,000
Main Body	8,000
First Reinforcements	800
Second Reinforcements	2,000
Third Reinforcements	1,800
Samoan Relief Force	500
Fourth Reinforcements	2,200
Fifth Reinforcements	2,000
Sixth Reinforcements	2,000
Extra Force	2,500
Seventh Reinforcements	2,000
Total in 10 months	25,800

Throughout this period the Dominion held a valuable reserve in hand, for the minimum age had been kept at twenty years. This excluded a fine body of young men between the age of eighteen and twenty, all of them well trained under the compulsory system; as grand a body of young soldiers as the world can show. Their number is estimated at 22,000, and over 90 per cent. of them have volunteered for service abroad. At the time of writing the question of lowering the age limit to eighteen was being considered in New Zealand, though the number of recruits of the standard age was still so satisfactory that the step was not necessary. New Zealand is preparing, like Australia,

The Canterbury Section of the New Zealand Expeditionary Force.

IN THE GREAT WAR

to send out five per cent. of its whole population to fight the battles of the Empire abroad ; that is a force of 50,000 men. The whole number of men of military age in the Dominion is less than 200,000.

Those who remain for the defence of the Southern nation are now busy in preparing munitions for the Great War. The factories of the young nations have already been converted into arsenals under the control of Munitions Boards, and hosts of volunteers are working long hours to supply the men of Australasia with every requisite for victory.

Lastly, Australasia has not forgotten that the duty of providing the Empire's food is one of the most important within her province. The year of the outbreak of war saw her producing industries hampered by a disastrous drought, so that the harvest failed and less than twenty per cent of the anticipated wheat supply was garnered. The year 1915 sees quite a different state of affairs ; bountiful rains have prepared the way for huge crops, and the farmers have sown lavishly, so that full advantage may be taken of this favourable state of affairs. When the harvest ripens, the call will be to the farms, and preparations are already being made for assistance from all quarters to the farmers who have parted with all their ablest assistants for the Empire's sake.

Australasia keeps a watchful eye on the gaps wherever they occur, and sets about filling them with a single-minded devotion to the great object which has obliterated all other consideration in the minds of those young nations of the peaceful lands beneath the Southern Cross.

HOW IT STRIKES AN AUSTRALASIAN

CHAPTER XI

HOW IT STRIKES AN AUSTRALASIAN

AMONG the most interesting contributions to British war literature have been the letters from the soldiers themselves, and the interviews with men from the Front that have found their way into print. Quite of equal interest and value to the views and impressions of Mr. Atkins are those of Tommy Cornstalk, who brings the new mind and a fine faculty of observation to the task of telling his people what he has seen and endured in that Old World at war, which is still only a dim vision to the bulk of the people of the Southern Nations.

Most of the men who have reached Great Britain for the period of their convalescence, are ready to vent in a most comical fashion their disgust with Fate. The trouble with them, almost to a man, is that they travelled half across the world, endured a course of assiduous training, and were then forced to retire from the fray without having fired a shot, or even seen a Turk. A group of fourteen men at one hospital averaged among them a stay of three days each at the Dardanelles. Two had been shot down in the boats and never set foot on shore; one veteran had been there eight days, before the bursting of a twelve-inch shell deprived him of an arm and a leg. The grim annoyance of such men that they cannot return to get "a bit of their own back" is only paralleled by the anxiety of the rest to make a speedy recovery with the same end in view.

But the most striking thing about their attitude of mind is the unanimity with which they apply the lessons of war, as they have seen it, to their own country. The same thing was noticeable about the men who returned from the African war; "no one can ever take Australia from us," they declared to a man, after their observation of the fight that the Boers had been able to put up against a greatly superior force in country of their own choice. And now they prefer to talk of the way in which Australia could be defended against an invader, if the Turks could hold up such a force as is employed in the reduction of Gallipoli.

Not that the scrubby heights and bristling ravines of Gaba Tepe appal them in the least. Their acquaintance with primitive Nature had prepared them for worse than that. They profess to know just how to get through, and are as full of wise theories and canny ideas as could be desired. Their minds hinge on possibilities and expedients;

the impossibilities and difficulties they leave to the croakers who stay at home. Their conversation is refreshing in its sane optimism, and its shrewd appreciation of the outstanding fact that difficulties only exist to be conquered.

It is better, however, to let the wounded Australian soldier talk for himself; for their letters tell most adequately what they think and their impressions of the new (to them) business of warfare. For instance, Private Hogarth writes :—" First we had to clamber up steep cliffs, and how we ever reached the top I don't know. I reckon we were stark, staring mad, and the more our fellows were knocked out the madder we became. Our bayonet exercise in Egypt was just the training we needed. Before the fight I thought it would be a dreadful sensation to kill a man, but when it came to the real thing I never gave that aspect of the matter a second thought. It was either kill or be killed, and in those circumstances it is certainly more pleasant to give than to receive. We lost a lot of men, but the Turks lost a lot, too. War is a great game, and I wouldn't have missed our scrap for all the tea in China. My great desire is to be back again, doing my bit to assist old England."

Next comes the experience of Lieutenant Manger, of the 5th Battalion :—" As soon as we landed we had to rush up a very steep hill and support the 3rd Brigade, who had driven the enemy back about

L

two miles. Then we came up and charged them back about a mile farther, but paid for our boldness, as their gun caught us in enfilade, and we found out what shrapnel was like. The Turks were very hard to find, as the country was very bushy. I knelt to use my glasses, and a sniper shot me in the leg, which broke my thigh. A poor chap who came to help me was also shot. I lay there, and the firing line advanced. I had been lying there about a quarter of an hour when I received another in the leg, and ten minutes later another in the thigh. Unfortunately I had to be there till night, but I spent my time in making a barricade of discarded kits, which saved me from more bullets.

"At nightfall four men gave me a hand and carried me out. We had not proceeded far before we found ourselves surrounded by Turks. The men dropped me and said they would come with help. I crawled into a big bush and lay there. The Turks were so close I could touch them. All night long I lay there under fire, and it was hell. The machine guns were something awful.

"In the morning the fleet started bombarding, and they gave it to them, but their guns were hard to find. The sound of the *Queen Elizabeth's* guns was awful, and made me jump every time. About four o'clock our chaps started again and charged the Turks off the ridge they were holding, and drove them on to the one on which I was hiding.

I was between two fires. The Turks had a machine gun within two yards of me, and I was unable to do anything, as I had lost all my equipment. Then our machine guns started on this ridge, and I can tell you I had to bury my head in the ground, but luckily I was not hit, although hundreds of bullets passed all around me. Then our fellows charged again and drove them away.

"There was one thing about the Turks—they never waited for our bayonets, but cleared. As soon as our chaps had occupied the ridge I was on the Turkish guns started again, and they swept the valley from one end to the other, and they could shoot, too. Then we brought up two guns to silence them, but our fellows did not stay there long, as their fire was too deadly, and every shot seemed to land on our guns, so they moved out. In the artillery duel I received a shrapnel wound on the arm, and damaged my thumb and second finger.

"About seven o'clock three men came along and dragged me out, and took me back to the doctor, who put my leg into temporary splints with a rifle and flag. I was thankful to be in, as I had been in the field and under fire for thirty-four hours."

Private Vernon Robertson, of Melbourne, says :—
"We had orders not to fire a shot, but to go right in with the bayonet. As the boats touched the bottom we were overboard chest deep, fixing bayonets as we rushed up the hills. The Turks won't wait

for the bayonet. I was in two bayonet charges, but never got within ten yards of a Turk. Major Fethers made good. He led us in two charges, but the enemy got him the third time. We had three days' hard going, and then I lost my eye, so crawled to the beach and was taken aboard the hospital ship and brought back to Cairo. I am likely to stay here two months and will then be sent back to Australia. During the three days I had a good innings, and got seven or eight Turks, so I have the satisfaction of having done my bit, and am not nearly so bad off as some others who have lost a leg or an arm. I saw a lyddite shell hit a Turk between the shoulders at 600 yards. It carried him some yards before exploding, and then killed eight or ten more. I also saw the *Queen Elizabeth* drop four 15-inchers into a battery. Guns, wheels and arms went about fifty feet into the air. An enemy battalion was forming up about a mile and a half away. An aeroplane gave ' *Lizzie* ' the range, and two 15-inch shrapnels just about annihilated the battalion, fully 800 Turks being left on the ground. In our two companies Captain Clements was the only officer unwounded on the Tuesday I was wounded."

Private R. Avery, of Port Albert, in a letter to his parents, says: "I only lasted two days over at the Gulf of Saros. I was all right in action—a bit hot, but that was all. The Turks are no class for us.

You can be sure we will be the winners. Bill [a brother] only lasted a few hours after landing, and got wounded in the arm. I hope to be going back in a week or two to have another fly at them."

Quartermaster-Sergeant Grayston says : "Myself and a few of C Company were mislaid. We were sent up on the left flank. Things were uncomfortably lively, but we had some real fun, and played the Turks a lively time. There were some twenty chaps in a small trench, and one after another we were wounded until we could hold out no longer, so I, with three others, retired a short way, and just as I was about to lower myself over the side of a steep gully on to a path below, shrapnel hit us, with the result that I suddenly disappeared, and landed in a sandy creek below. I thought every bone in my body was broken. On attempting to stand I found that all my serious injuries were either a broken or badly sprained ankle and an injured back. I crawled and was assisted on to the beach, and then to the hospital boat, and later on deposited at the hospital in Alexandria. The quicker I get back to the firing line, the better I will like it. I believe four out of our six officers are killed, leaving only two in C Company."

Private F. C. Howgate, of Clifton Hill, writes from the base hospital, Egypt : "Just a few lines to say I am still living, and glad to be able to say so. Since joining the army I have felt bloodthirsty and was delighted when we went on the warpath, because it eased my mind considerably. We landed on the shores of the peninsula on a beautiful morning, covered by the heavy fire from our warships, and met the enemy entrenched right on the shore, We were received by a storm of bullets, but when they saw cold steel that was enough. They left everything and flew, but we were unable to catch them. We established ourselves well inland by noon, and held our position until I was put out by a shell which lifted me and put me about twenty yards farther back. The sensation was simply awful; I got ripped in the back, and it was like running a razor down one's spine. Now, I am glad to say, I hope to be about soon and have another go at them, as I must get a bit of my own back. The most wonderful of all sights is ' Our *Lizzie*.' She looks only a handful, but when she puts a ' broad ' on to a hill, its shape is entirely altered for about 100 feet. On Monday I saw a shell of hers get fairly on to a big gun, which was lifted to the height of about twenty feet."

Corporal A. L. Gray, of Tamworth, writes: " Every man fought against great odds. Still, there is for a man with grit the name of Australia to uphold, and they did it finely. We landed at 6 a.m., and it was well past the dinner hour when I got my bit of lead in the upper part of the arm, entering near the shoulder, and coming out the other side, just grazing the bone. It is a week to-day, and next Sunday it will be better, making it possible for me to go back again. The chaps in hospital (Heliopolis Hotel) are in best of spirits, the one-arm brigades and the dot-and-dash legs included; but you cannot and never will see a brotherhood like that of Australian troops."

Private R. J. Vidler, of West Tamworth, says: "We are up to all the dodges that you can imagine, and if some of us are going under you can imagine it will be desperate to the utmost. We will sell our lives as dearly as possible, and if any of us die fighting, it will be fighting in a good cause, and all of us are determined to carry this little job through."

Private Harry Hoy, writing to his mother from Malta, laments the fact that he was wounded in the left arm very shortly after he landed at the Dardanelles. "I had not got a good start on," he says, "when I got a bit of Turkish delight in the left arm. We were landing under a shower of bullets, and shrapnel that reminded me of a hailstorm. Still, I never saw a gamer lot in my life. Personally, I felt like I used to when going on a football field, and was very disappointed at having to retire so soon. Nevertheless, I hope to last a lot longer when I get back next time."

Now, these letters, and the hundreds of similar ones, deal mainly with essentials. If one contrasts them with those of the German soldier, which contain endless references to food and drink, or with the more cheerful jocular letters of Mr. Atkins, or with the frequent patriotic references of the Frenchman, the grim practicality of them becomes apparent. The wounded Australian wants to get back and get it over, for the sake of Australia, and "good old England." That is how it strikes an Australasian.

THE MAN WHO WASN'T LET

CHAPTER XII

THE MAN WHO WASN'T LET

PERHAPS he was Let, eventually. But when I met him he was emphatically the man who wasn't Let to fight.

I met him in London, a tall, well-set Australian, wearing the all-wool khaki of the Commonwealth and the neat leather cap of the Australian Divisional Supply Column. In his own words he was a "Leatherhead." He was a thirteen-stone man, but without a spare ounce of flesh on him anywhere; one could quite believe him when he said he was "as strong as a Monaro steer." And over his right eye he wore a pink celluloid patch.

This decoration moved my curiosity, for I knew the Leatherheads had not taken part in the Dardanelles fighting but were at that time destined for very active service elsewhere. In fact, they were on the very eve of embarking; therefore I opened a conversation by asking if he were off "to the front."

"No, worse luck," he said, "I'm the only man

staying behind. They won't let me fight." This with some bitterness.

A little sympathy, judiciously expressed, started him talking; and in the monotonous drawl affected by the men of the Australian bush—natural to them, it may be—he unfolded a strange story of his wanderings in search of a fight. He told me who he was, and what he was; they are not essential to the point of his story. It is enough to say that he sacrificed a very good income and excellent prospects to join the Australian Expeditionary Force.

"You see," he said, "I've got only one eye, my left; but it's a good one. I lost the other eight years ago—mining. Since then I've come to the conclusion that a man doesn't need two eyes, except in case of accident, like mine. I had a glass eye fixed up in Sydney, just like the other one, and you couldn't tell the difference; well, when I tell you, you'll know that you couldn't.

"I was always fond of soldiering, and joined the militia. I got my musketry certificate, so that shows you a man with one eye can shoot as well as any man with two, and a sight better than most of them. I've done some 'roo shooting, too, and a fellow that can knock over an old man running at three hundred with a worn Martini, don't want any spare eyes.

"When I was in Sydney I learned to drive a

motor-car, and never had any trouble. A man who can take a fast car through the Sydney traffic don't want to worry about being shy of one eye. And nobody ever noticed; I used to get on well with girls, and all that; and they're the first to grumble if a man's got anything wrong with him.

"I've seen a lot of bush life; done thirty miles a day with a big swag in my time, and was never sick or sorry in my life. All this leads up to what I'm going to tell you.

"Naturally I volunteered when the war came, having no one dependent on me. Besides, I never liked Germans. I passed the medical examination all right; and they are mighty particular over there. Of course the doctor never tumbled to my glass eye, and there was nothing else the matter with me.

"When they found I could drive a motor, they put me among the Leatherheads; but I had to pass a driving test first, and that was no child's play. But still nobody tumbled to my glass eye, and I wasn't saying anything. I went into camp in the Domain, and everything was all right till they inoculated me against typhoid.

"It took pretty bad with me; they tell me that's a good sign. But I was feverish and felt rotten, and had to go into hospital. When the doctor came round the second day, I had a dirty tongue and a temperature, and he whistled a bit.

"'Let's look at your eye,' he said; and before I knew what he was after, he had pulled back my bottom lid to see if there was any inflammation there. Of course, my old glass eye rolled out on the pillow.

"You oughter seen that doctor jump. He went quite white in the face, too. Well, there was nobody about, and presently he burst out laughing, which I took to be a good sign. So I said, 'Are you going to be a sport, doctor? No one knows but you, and there's no need for you to know.'

"'Are you sure nobody knows?' he asked, still laughing fit to burst. 'Not a soul,' I told him. He tried the eye. 'Wonderful,' he says; 'I don't know either.' So I got away with the Contingent."

"When our boys got off at Egypt we came on here, because our motor outfit was no manner of use in the sand there. We never went to the Dardanelles for the same reason; but have been five long months in camp at Romsey. All that time I've been doing the same work as the rest; transporting gravel in the motor wagon, and all the rest of it. And not a soul ever tumbled to my glass eye.

"Then it was settled that we should be sent—somewhere. But before we could go, the whole lot of us had to go through a fresh medical examination; British Army doctors this time. I was going to chance it; and I don't think they would ever have found me out. But you never know what you're doing with these English doctors; they're not reasonable chaps like in Australia, as you shall see. And I didn't want to get the C.O. into trouble; he's a grand chap, Tunbridge.

"So when the doctor came to me, I made a clean breast of it; you ought to have seen the C.O.'s face. He was dead surprised; so would any one be. But the doctor turned nasty. 'I can't pass you,' he said. 'A one-eyed man driving a car! Disgraceful!' And so on.

"Nothing I could say or do was any use; I was rejected. I'm as strong as a Monaro steer, and my eye is as good as three ordinary ones. But— no good.

"So I got a week's leave, and went off to see a bit of England. Down at Southampton I fell in with some Canadians; real good sorts, they were. We had a drink or two, and I found they were off to the front that very night. Here was a chance! I fixed things up with them, and borrowed a slouch hat; then I made my cap into a neat parcel, and left it at the railway parcels office. There was I, as good a Canuck as any of them. Except that I had 'Australia' on my shoulders instead of 'Canada,' but that didn't matter.

"It was dark when we lined up on the pier and they called the roll. I got into the back row, and they called everybody's name but mine; and everybody said 'Here,' except me. Bit neglectful, I call it; but I was there all right. 'Australia *will* be there.'

"We got over to Havre, and everybody was fussing about his dunnage, so I fussed about mine. Of course I didn't have any, but I gave such a good description of it that to get rid of me the fellow said, 'It's over there.' So I got on to the train, and up to the front at a place I think they called Dickiesborough. It sounded like that.

"We were all billeted in a big barn with stacks of grub; and next evening my pals were detailed to go out into the trenches. I got hold of a rifle and some ammunition; there was no difficulty. And I went off with them.

"It was dusk, and about 400 yards from the communication trench we all went down on our hands and knees and crawled. I crawled, too, and kept low, as they told me, when we got to the communication trench; and presently we were all snug in the first line of trenches.

"Then my luck turned. Along came a Canadian officer, to inspect. 'Are you all right here, sergeant?' he says. 'How many men have you got?' 'Twenty-one, sir,' says the sergeant in quite a little voice. 'Twenty, you mean.' 'No, sir, twenty-one. There's a long Australian galoot here, that wants to have a shot at the Germans, so we brought him with us.'

"Now if that'd been an English officer there'd

have been a row, and I should have been shot, or something. But this captain says, 'Here, that won't do. Let's have a look at you.' So he ran the rule over me, and examined my papers, and felt my khaki—he even felt my khaki! He knew a bit, that Canuck captain.

"Then he said, 'I believe you are telling the truth, but I can't have you here. You'll be getting wounded or something; you're just the sort of fool that would.' He spoke very nice. 'You wouldn't have the sense to get killed,' he said. 'You'd be wounded, and I couldn't account for you. So, get,' he says.

"'How am I to get out?' I asked. 'The same way you got in,' he says, very short. 'And where am I to go?' And I wouldn't like to tell you where he told me to go to.

"Well, I stooped and went back along the communication trench. I wasn't going to draw the fire on the boys who were in the firing line. But when I got to the end of it, I stood up, and put my fingers in my mouth and I whistled as loud as I could. I couldn't shoot at the Germans, but I did want a bit of fighting. I put my hands in my pockets and strolled back over that ground where we'd been crawling; and I whistled 'The Wild Colonial Boy.' Nobody took a bit of notice.

"I slept in the billet that night, and had a real good breakfast; then the wounded began to come in. There was a pretty lively scrap through the night; of course I slept through it all—just my luck. I made myself useful—stretcher-bearing and what not. But I could see that if I stayed there, I'd only get myself into trouble, and somebody else, too, very likely.

"I went to the little base hospital, and I said, 'Can you give me an eyeshade. My eye is paining me.' And they gave me this. They were just making up a hospital train for the coast, so I chucked away my glass eye—I was disgusted with it anyhow —and put on the shade. Then I got on the train as one of the poor wounded.

"Presently another doctor comes round—this place seems stiff with doctors—and examined me. 'That's getting on nicely,' he says, looking very hard at me. 'Yes, doctor,' I says, as if I was in pain. Of course he must have seen there was something wrong, but he was too busy to worry about a little thing like that.

"We had a pleasant journey down : nurses fussing around, and so on. And what do you think I struck on the ship ? 'Another blooming doctor!' (unconsciously quoting Kipling).

"He was so pleased with my quick recovery that he brought an assistant to look at me. They seemed quite dazed about it, but they were busy men: plenty to keep them occupied without troubling about me, which is just as it should be.

"I got my cap at Southampton, and joined up with my old corps. No fighting for me.

"Now I've got to send in my papers. But I've not come 12,000 miles for a fight with the Germans to go home without firing a shot. I'm getting a new eye made here in London; I've seen it in the rough and it's a boshter, the real thing. They know how to make them here.

"And I'm going to have it riveted in, and soldered down and fastened in its place with concrete; then I'm going to enlist with Kitchener's boys. If they find me out, they can only jug me. Do you think they would?"

* * * * *

I could not tell him. It is more than likely. A strong man with a glass eye, who insists on fighting the enemy at a time like this, is apt to be considered a danger in this country. Especially when he has an undetectable glass eye.

SAID AN AUSTRALIAN OFFICER

CHAPTER XIII

SAID AN AUSTRALIAN OFFICER

"FRATERNIZING with the Indians!" chuckled the Australian officer, as he laid down a London evening paper which had been expressing satisfaction at the fact that Australasians and Indians were fighting side by side before Sari Bair. "The last fraternizing I saw was being done by a young officer of the A.S.C. He was brandishing something that looked like a pick handle (of course he never used it), and demanding a lost transport mule in a fervid mixture of Arabic, Turkish, and Never-Never talk from the Back of Nowhere.

"You see, these Indians are fatalists to a man; they think that if they are to be hit, they must be, and there's an end of it. The consequence is, they take no care of themselves; and that wouldn't matter so much, if they'd only take reasonable care of the mules. Mules are precious, but they take their mules anywhere, and lose them. Hence the fraternizing. 'Where's my mule, son of Belial?' this chap was shouting; and the other things he was saying made even a little middie look shocked.

"We never got tired of those middies. You'd see a pinnace coming up to the beach under shell-fire, and a little chap of fourteen talking to the boat's crew like a Yanko bullock driver. The big sailor men were all grinning with sheer delight at the snap of the boys, who didn't seem to know what fear was. I tried some middy's talk on my men once, and startled them down to their bones. They thought about it for half a minute, and then one fellow asked me where I was hit.

"When we go back to Australia, the Australian language will be richer for a word or two of Arabic, that will go there to stay. We have made a regular battle cry of 'Imshi Yalla,' which means 'Get on with it' as far as we can make out. Then there's 'Mafish,' meaning 'Finished.' It was the last word on the lips of many a good man in those days at the end of last April. The ordinary camp greeting is 'Sayeeda'—'Good day,' or 'How d'ye do?' as I take it. There's a word or two more, but there is no need to translate them. They are useful words.

"The Turks are fine fellows. People ask me if they were not very cruel; and I hear all sorts of rumours about mutilations, and so on. There is not one word of truth in it. The story went round that one well-known Australian officer had

Colonel Sir Newton Moore, in charge of the Australasian Depôt at Weymouth

been found hideously mutilated; and I happen to be in a position to contradict that story point-blank. When the armistice was declared at the end of the battle of Quinn's Post, it was my sorrowful duty to identify and bury the body of that officer. He had not a mark on him, except the honourable wound that caused his death. Dr. Springthorpe, who is the chief Australian medical officer in Egypt, has assured me that no case of mutilation has been treated in the hospitals there; which contradicts some very circumstantial stories that have found their way into print, both here and in Australia.

"That armistice was a funny business. Of course, the only people with any business between the lines were the Red Cross people, but no sooner had the armistice begun than a whole lot of German officers in Turkish uniforms stepped out, and began to make the best use of their opportunities for taking observations. The only counter for that was that we should go out too, and we did so. The Germans were as grumpy as pigs about it, but the Turkish officers turned out to be fine gentlemen. Soon I was swopping cigarettes with them, and we were carrying on a conversation in bad French, eked out with scraps of all other tongues. They were quite jolly fellows, and brave fighters into the bargain.

"It was during that armistice that I saw a German

officer talking to some Turkish soldiers with a shovel. They did not move quickly enough to suit him, I suppose, and he laid into them with it. He was not particular whether the flat or the edge of it struck them, so long as he did not miss altogether. I said to my fellows, 'How should we get on, if I did that to you?' and they only scowled. Two of them went out a night or two afterwards, and came back with some buttons they said were his. I don't know.

"Yes, the Turks are brave men, and brave women, too. I saw with my own eyes one sniper brought in, all covered with twigs and painted green in the face. This sniper was smoking a cigarette presented by one of our fellows, and when a couple more added a pat on the back, and said 'Cheero,' the sniper burst into tears. It was a young Turkish girl. Upon my word, I saw the thing happen. She had provisions for three weeks and a thousand rounds, and as nice a little cubbyhole as you ever saw to hide in. I don't know what became of her, but I can vouch for what I am telling you being true.

"We will always remember the Turks kindly for one thing. We lost General Bridges, our chief; who fell to a sniper's bullet in Monash Gully (The Valley of Death), when on his round of inspection. He refused to be carried down to the sea-front, because of the danger his bearers would have to risk. Of course, no one would hear of such nonsense; and he was carried. He was taken slowly through all the most dangerous windings of the valley; yet not a single Turk fired a shot. That stands to their credit with every Australian on the peninsula.

"There are lots of funny things I could tell you, but you might think I was qualifying for the post of 'First Man.' The First Man ? Oh, that's a title any fellow gets in the trenches who begins to tell tall yarns. You see, in the first days there was a lot of talk about who was the first man ashore. He turned up here, there, and everywhere; everybody knew him. I believe there were some fights about it. Then some fellows out at Courtney's had a big tin medal made, and whenever any one began boasting, he would be presented with this medal, inscribed, 'For the First Man Ashore.' Nearly every battalion has one of those medals now.

"There were three brothers in my company, all as brave as lions. Fred, the youngest of the three, was reckless with it; and his two brothers were always worrying about him. One day he was hit on the shoulder, and when they saw him go down, one brother shouted to the other, 'Thank Heaven, young Fred's got it!' Of course, we all knew what he meant—he was pleased the boy had got off with a light wound—but it made the fellows laugh. After that, whenever one of them was hit, officer talking to some Turkish soldiers with a shovel. They did not move quickly enough to suit him, I suppose, and he laid into them with it. He was not particular whether the flat or the edge of it struck them, so long as he did not miss altogether. I said to my fellows, ' How should we get on, if I did that to you ? ' and they only scowled. Two of them went out a night or two afterwards, and came back with some buttons they said were his. I don't know.

"Yes, the Turks are brave men, and brave women, too. I saw with my own eyes one sniper brought in, all covered with twigs and painted green in the face. This sniper was smoking a cigarette presented by one of our fellows, and when a couple more added a pat on the back, and said 'Cheero,' the sniper burst into tears. It was a young Turkish girl. Upon my word, I saw the thing happen. She had provisions for three weeks and a thousand rounds, and as nice a little cubbyhole as you ever saw to hide in. I don't know what became of her, but I can vouch for what I am telling you being true.

"We will always remember the Turks kindly for one thing. We lost General Bridges, our chief; who fell to a sniper's bullet in Monash Gully (The Valley of Death), when on his round of inspection. He refused to be carried down to the sea-front, because of the danger his bearers would have to risk. Of course, no one would hear of such nonsense; and he was carried. He was taken slowly through all the most dangerous windings of the valley; yet not a single Turk fired a shot. That stands to their credit with every Australian on the peninsula.

"There are lots of funny things I could tell you, but you might think I was qualifying for the post of ' First Man.' The First Man ? Oh, that's a title any fellow gets in the trenches who begins to tell tall yarns. You see, in the first days there was a lot of talk about who was the first man ashore. He turned up here, there, and everywhere; everybody knew him. I believe there were some fights about it. Then some fellows out at Courtney's had a big tin medal made, and whenever any one began boasting, he would be presented with this medal, inscribed, 'For the First Man Ashore.' Nearly every battalion has one of those medals now.

"There were three brothers in my company, all as brave as lions. Fred, the youngest of the three, was reckless with it; and his two brothers were always worrying about him. One day he was hit on the shoulder, and when they saw him go down, one brother shouted to the other, ' Thank Heaven, young Fred's got it ! ' Of course, we all knew what he meant—he was pleased the boy had got off with a light wound—but it made the fellows laugh. After that, whenever one of them was hit, he'd shout, ' Thank Heaven, young Fred's got it ! ' and then lie down and curse.

"This brother was the coolest customer in the trench, and that was saying something. He was a crack shot, and a great hand at destroying Turkish periscopes. Smashing the business end of a periscope with a rifle bullet, even at short range, is not so easy as it sounds; for the observers keep them moving about erratically, so that it is something like a very small disappearing target. But Bill nailed one nearly every time he shot, and the Turks used to chatter with rage at each loss. I don't think they had too many of them.

"They broke a good many of our periscopes in the same fashion; and the broken glass used to fly about in a very nasty way. I had five men cut about the face and head on one day, through their periscopes being broken at observation work. Then we improvised a sort of safety helmet out of half a kerosene tin, and put an end to that trouble We tried the new steel embrasures at Quinn's Post, but I consider them sheer death traps, where the trenches are so close to those of the enemy as twenty yards. The fellows who used them at a distance of 150 or 200 yards spoke most highly of them; but where I was, a gap in the sandbags served much better.

"The Turk is a punctual beast. We used to time our watches every evening by the first shell of the evening bombardment, which invariably came along at ten minutes past six. On the night of May 18, that first shell was followed by 170 others before it had gone seven o'clock, which was pretty good going. The armistice of the 20th May was supposed to end at four o'clock in the afternoon, and at one minute past, along came the first shell, just to show us that our friend Abdul had his eye on the clock.

"It came from an entirely new direction, too, which showed that the opportunity for observation afforded by the armistice had not been wasted. But I think we were able to show that we had not shut our eyes to things that were easily noticeable. They certainly did not gain much in the exchanges over that armistice. It's all in the game, after all. There has been little said about the work of the Australasian artillery, and for the very best of reasons. But the gunners, and especially the New Zealanders, will get their due later on.

"There is one New Zealander who is a perfect marvel with a machine gun—Captain Wallingford, a champion shot. He got the Military Cross for his great work on the opening days, so one can speak about him. A machine gun soon draws fire, and it was no uncommon thing for the whole of a section to go down soon after a machine gun opened fire. The way he shifted his gun about in unfamiliar, broken country, through thick scrub and in the dark, was something to dream about. He had a sharpshooting section, too, that was death on snipers, and cleared a whole section of the front in very quick time.

"Colonel Owen's men (the 3rd Battalion) always call him 'Old Never-Retire.' I asked one of them the reason, and he said that on the morning of the first landing the Colonel had to take his fellows up a very steep bit of cliff, almost inaccessible. His position worried the Admiral so much that he signalled that he had better retire, and try farther to the right. The Colonel turned on the chap who brought the message and said, 'My compliments to the Admiral, and tell him I'll see him damned first.' I don't know whether that is true, for I never had the chance of testing it. But his men swear to it.

"The loudest cheer I heard from the trenches was given to a sergeant whose name I never found out; but I know he was a Western Australian. Two sharpshooters had crawled out about thirty yards for a better shot, and had gone down together; one with a broken arm, and the other with a shot through the thigh. They lay there, with bullets kicking up the dust around them, when this sergeant went out with a rope. He tied it round the waist of the man with the broken arm, who was dragged to the trench, yelling with pain. Then he picked the other fellow up on his back, and brought him in through a perfect rain of bullets. He never had a scratch. It was away to the left of me, and below me, and I saw it all through my glasses, and heard the cheers, as if I were sitting in the circle at a theatre. We found by signal he was unhurt, but could not get his name.

"There were two platoons away on the right who distinguished themselves by getting farther inland than any one else. Not many of them returned to tell the tale, but it was a queer story. They lost all their officers and most of the non-coms. quite early on. The rest only knew they were there to take a hill, and so they took one. Then, for fear that might be the wrong hill, they took another. That set them off taking all the hills in sight, a pretty tall order. They only stopped when they blundered on to the Turkish camp; the wonder is that any of them ever got back.

"I wish the Turks were as cleanly as they are brave and punctual. They keep their trenches in a filthy condition. I know, because I occupied one for half a day. We were told to take it; and that was all right, with the help of the bayonet. We stayed there half a day, and were quite glad when we were ordered back again. It was dangerous enough there; but, for the moment, the danger was nothing compared to the stench and vermin. We lost a lot of men getting out; but were told

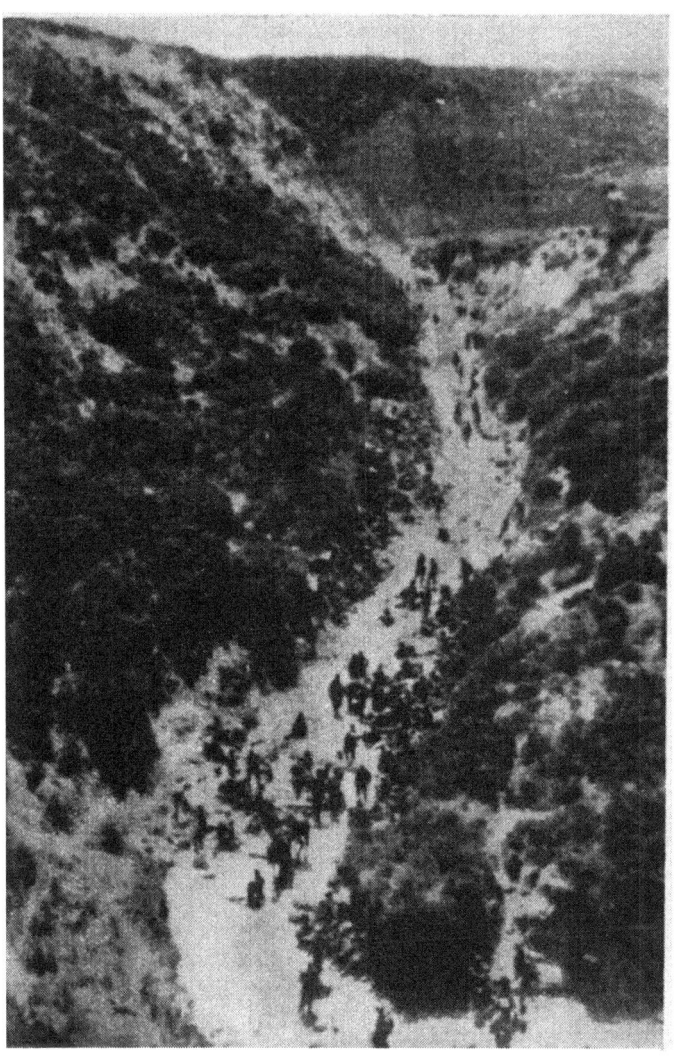

The Valley of Death.

prisoners taken is not large; there is so much cover there that it is a risky game making prisoners.

"There are plenty of Germans there; the artillery officers and the whole of the machine gun sections are Germans. They wear Turkish uniforms, and are what we call 'Pointers' in Australia. During the armistice, they were trying very hard to get their rifles away with bolts and all, back to the Turkish lines. They were supposed to take the rifle and leave the bolt, thus making the weapon useless. I had to stop quite a number who were sneaking off with complete rifles; there was a bit of a row about one man, because I happened to hit him with my fist. I could not make him understand what I wanted by any other means. But there are fewer Germans now than when we first landed."

THE HEART OF EMPIRE STIRRED

CHAPTER XIV

THE HEART OF EMPIRE STIRRED

IF Australasia sought reward for the devotion and heroism displayed in the time of the peril of the whole Empire, other than the consciousness of duty done ungrudgingly and continuously, that reward has surely been accorded by the proud Mother Country. From the King himself down to the humblest of his subjects, Britons have shared with the Southern nations all the sentiments that have been elicited by the performance of Australasians in their first great essay at waging war.

London, the very Heart of the Empire, has been from time to time profoundly stirred as the news of some exploit by the representatives of Australasia has been received. It laughed with glee at the discomfiture of the boasting captain of the *Emden*, and gladly recognized the maiden prowess of the young Australian fleet. It thrilled with sympathetic pride for the great charge up the cliff at Gaba Tepe; and accepted without cavil the generous estimate of one of the foremost British war correspondents:

"It is certainly the most remarkable climb in the history of war since Wolfe stormed the heights of Quebec."

Most grateful of all to hundreds of sorrowing hearts in Australasia, London turned aside from its own countless griefs to mourn with Australasia the loss of the brave dead from the South. Nothing was more eloquent of the profound stir at the Heart of the Empire than that solemn memorial service to the Australasian dead held in St. Paul's Cathedral on the evening of June 15, 1915. In that sacred building, where repose the mortal remains of Nelson, Wellington, and many another great one who died for the Empire that Australasia is so proud to serve, there gathered an assemblage of mourners come to pay a spontaneous tribute to the brave young men who had laid down their lives for a great ideal. The King was represented there; and the Colonial Secretary, Mr. Bonar Law, himself born in the Dominions Overseas, attended on behalf of the Government. Great men and noble women of all shades of opinion thronged in the aisles to pay their tribute to the heroes dead, but never to be forgotten. And the citizens of the greatest city of the world were represented by their Lord Mayor, as by many a humble sympathizer who gained a place in the thronged building as a mark of loving kindness to mourners so far away, yet so near to the Empire's heart.

Some hundreds of Australasian soldiers were there—men who had fought bravely by the side of the dead ones the Empire was mourning, and had themselves sustained grave wounds in that Empire's defence. The rays of the setting sun lit their dull khaki as it lit the brilliant scarlet uniform of the bandsmen of the Grenadier Guards. The hush of true mourning was on the mighty building, and every sentence of the impressive sermon preached by the Archbishop of Canterbury could be heard in the farthest corner.

The Primate, who took for his text St. John xv. 13—" Greater love hath no man than this, that a man lay down his life for his friends"—said :

" We are met to-night for a definite and a very sacred purpose. Here at the centre and hub of the Empire's life, we desire to thank God together for the splendid devotion of our brothers from Australia and New Zealand, who in the cause whereto we as a people have set our hand regarded not their lives unto the death. It is as Christians that we are here to-night, as men and women, that is, who hold definitely to certain great truths, and are not ashamed to say so. We are firm in the belief that the bit of life which we spend here— be it, on man's reckoning, long or short—is not all. This part of it is of vital moment. It is a great opportunity. It is a high trust. It is capable of splendid use. But it is quite certainly—as we

Christians view it—not all. It is part of something larger, something with a nobler range.

"And Christ has to do with all of it, here and hereafter, and He made it clear that in His eyes it matters vitally how we spend and use this part of it, how we devote it, how, if need calls, we lay it down. He spoke of those things to His friends on the night before He died, when the full moonlight was flooding the upper room, and He was bidding them farewell. This is only a part, He told them, but it ought to be a glad and bright part, of the larger life. And its gladness, its joy, would depend, in each man's case, upon whether he had learned the greatness of its value as something to be used, devoted, laid down, if need be, for the sake of other people. That was the key to His life, His joy; it would be the key to theirs. He bid them try to understand it so. That, He says, was why He had been reminding them of what He had come to do. 'These things I have spoken unto you.' Why? 'That my joy'—the joy of ready sacrifice for others, the true test of love—'might remain in you, and that your joy might be full. . . . Greater love hath no man than this, that a man lay down his life for his friends.'

"You see, my brothers and sisters, how all that bears upon the thought which is just now sweeping across and through us as a people, and which helps to crowd these seats to-night. We want, as Christians, to say together in St. Paul's this evening that we honestly, deliberately, believe these fearful perils, these wounded or stricken bodies of our best and bravest, these saddened hearths and darkened homes, to be worth while. And if they are ' worth while,' they are right. The offering, terrible as it is, ought to be made without reserve for the sake of what is, as we deliberately judge, the cause of truth and honour, the cause of good faith and ordered liberty among the peoples of Europe and of the world. It is a duty grave, inspiring, urgent, which ought to rally us every one.

"I do not pause to ask whether the sacrifice would be worth while if this life on earth were all. I think it would, but I need not dwell upon that now. It is as Christians that we meet to-night, and to a belief in the larger life lying behind and around and beyond what we see, a Christian, however bewildered he feel about how it can all work out, is clearly pledged. Most of us, I suppose, whisper longingly at times, perhaps in hours like this we say out, almost imperatively, 'We want to know more, a great deal more, about the nature, even the particulars, of that other life. They are so difficult to picture in plain words in their relation to what we are familiar with here, and the more we try to work out the vision the more bewildered we grow. Is there nothing in the Bible to tell us plainly how it all will be, or, rather, how it all is ? '

"The answer is not difficult. The Bible does not furnish any such detailed answer to our longing inquiry. It gives us unchallengeably the sure and certain faith in that greater life. That faith underlies as a firm basis the whole New Testament. But neither in vision nor parable is the veil wholly drawn aside. As the old seer said, 'The secret things belong unto the Lord our God,' and these are among the secret things. We know little; but what we do know we know for certain. Remember this. We are loyal to our Lord Christ, Whose life was the light of men, and Whose words and teaching are our strength and stay. We believe Him whatever else we doubt.

"Now, take any section, say, any five chapters of the Gospel story, about what He said and did. Read them anew, trying, as you read, to destroy or do without the basis and background of that other larger life, and you will find the account, I do not hesitate to say, simply unintelligible as words of truth. The belief, the knowledge as to that larger life underlies and colours the whole, and makes it literally true to say that if we are Christians, if we are believers in Him at all, that certitude which He gives us is and must be ours. Without it you cannot advance a yard in the understanding of what His Gospel meant. On that last evening He told them He was going away. But why? 'I go to prepare a place for you . . . that where I am there ye may be also.' That is to say, 'You are to live on and to work on.' What meaning else for some of the most uplifting and inspiring of the parables which He had given them ? 'Thou hast been faithful over a few things, I will make thee ruler over many things : enter thou into the joy of thy Lord.' What meaning for the story of the rich man and Lazarus ? What meaning for the words of definite and uplifting promise to the thief upon the cross ? 'To-day shalt thou be with Me in Paradise.' And so we might run on. Brothers, to us Christians it is not a hope only, it is a sure and certain hope.

" It is well to remember that this is so when in the cloudy and dark day we are fretting and wondering and seem only to stretch lame hands and grope. But we perhaps ask : 'Why, why, this absence of some clear exposition of it all ? ' Well, what if, to our present faculties, such knowledge would be literally unconveyable in terms that we could understand ? Many here are familiar with—some perhaps have ere now quoted—a certain picture-parable which belongs specially to this Cathedral. Just two centuries ago, the Christian philosopher, George Berkeley, a singularly clear thinker, was standing, as he tells us, in St. Paul's Cathedral, where he noticed a little fly crawling on one of those great pillars. He had been uplifted in thought by the overwhelming grandeur of symmetry and design in pier and arch and dome and gallery, and the relation of each part to each and to the whole. And then he watched the little crawling fly, to whom no understanding of the whole was possible, who could see nothing of its harmonies, and to whom, as he puts it, 'nothing could appear but the small inequalities in the surface of the hewn stone, which in the view of the insect seemed so many deformed rocks and precipices.' Here, he thought, is the likeness of each human being as he creeps along. The sorrow which, like some dreadful precipice, interrupts our life, may turn out to be nothing but the joining or cement which binds the portions and sections of the greater life into one beautiful and harmonious whole. The dark path may be but the curve which, in the full daylight of a brighter world, will be seen to be the inevitable span of some majestic arch. 'Now I know in part,' and what a very little part it is, 'but then shall I know even as also I am known.'

" Does all that seem poor and vague and cheerless to the young wife across whose sunny home the dark shadow has fallen, to the mother who, through all her brave faith, looks out dazed and dry-eyed upon the shattering of the hopes which had been her daily happiness and strength ? The message is not—or it will not always be—vague and cheerless if the firm and even glad courage with which a few months ago she offered willingly what she loved best on earth, be transmuted now into trustful prayer and into loyal proud thankfulness for duty nobly done, and into quiet awaiting of the ampler life beyond, with the answer it must bring in His good time to the questions of the aching heart. Which of us but has been inspired already by what Our Father has shown us to be possible—nay, rather to be actually attained—in the ennobled lives of those whom He 'out of weakness has made strong.' There is, for we are seeing it every day, as real a heroism of the stricken home as the heroism of the shell-swept trench, or of the quivering deck. For that, too, for those brave women in England, or in the Southern Seas, we are upon our knees to-night, thanking 'the God of all comfort Who comforteth us in all our tribulation, that we may be able to comfort them which are in any trouble by the comfort wherewith we ourselves are comforted of God.'

"But in this great gathering to-night we want another note besides that. We must have the triumph-note for those whose self-sacrifice has meant so much to their country and to those who honour them. It has been theirs, in enthusiastic eager self-surrender, to reach what Christ marks as the highest grade of human love. 'Greater love hath no man than this, that a man lay down his life for his friends.' Gratefully and reverently we remember that heroism now. That is what brings us here for thanksgiving and for prayer. Among the lives laid down could be found, as always, bright examples of the young leadership to which we had looked for upholding among their fellows the spirit which sets manliness upon the surest basis, the basis of personal loyalty to Christ. For those lives and for the footprints which they have left upon the sands of time we give praise to God to-day.

"But it would be unnatural, untrue, to claim for all who thus gave their lives in their country's cause, the character of stainless purity, or of the saintliness which we sing of in our hymns. Some of them, perhaps many of them, were not 'saints' at all. They were manly sons of the greatest Empire in the world. They were brave and buoyant, with plenty of the faults and failures which go so often with high spirit. They need, as we shall need, forgiveness and cleansing and new opportunity, and they are in their Father's keeping, and He knows and cares. Be it theirs—shall we not pray it with all our hearts ?—be it theirs, under His good hand, to pass onward in the new and larger life from strength to strength.

> Blow, trumpets, all your exultations blow!
> For never shall their aureoled presence lack:
> I see them muster in a gleaming row,
> With ever-youthful brows that nobler show:
> We find in our dull road their shining track;
>   In every nobler mood
> We feel the orient of their spirit glow,
> Part of our life's unalterable good.

"Do these words seem too high for what we are remembering? I think not. This vast war, without parallel in history for the horrible scale and sweep of its devastating bloodshed, is unparalleled in other ways as well. The feat of arms which was achieved on the rocky beach and scrub-grown cliff of the Gallipoli Peninsula in the grey dawn of St. Mark's Day, April 25, was a feat, we are assured, whose prowess has never been outshone, has scarcely ever been rivalled, in military annals. As the open boats, under a hail from hidden guns, poured out their men in thousands on the beach, below perpendicular cliffs of tangled scrub, the task of breasting those heights looked, to many expert eyes, a sheer impossibility. But by the dauntless gallantry of brave men the impossible feat was accomplished, and the record of those hours and of the days which followed is now a portion of our Empire's heritage for ever.

"And who did it? It was not the product of the long discipline of some veteran corps of soldiers. It was mainly the achievement of men from sheep-stations in the Australian Bush, or from the fields or townships of New Zealand, who a few short months ago had no dream of warfare as, like other civilians, they went about their ordinary work. But the call rang out, and the response was ready, and the result is before us all. ' I have never,' says one competent observer after the battle, ' I have never seen the like of these wounded Australians in war before. They were happy because they knew they had been tried for the first time, and had not been found wanting. No finer feat of arms has been performed during the war than this sudden landing in the dark, the storming of the heights, and, above all, the holding on to the position thus won while reinforcements were poured from the transports.'

"It is high praise, but the witness is true, and those Australians and New Zealanders are enrolled among the champions whom the Empire, for generations to come, will delight to honour. One of the best traits of all is the generous tribute given by each group to the indomitable valour of the rest. To quote from the private letter of a young New Zealander : 'The Australians were magnificent, and deserve every good word that is said of them.' And all unite to praise the officers, midshipmen, and men who formed the beach parties in that eventful landing, each boat, we are reminded, 'in charge of a young midshipman, many of whom have come straight from Dartmouth after only a couple of terms.'

"But of necessity it was at fearful cost that these gallant deeds were done, and the great roll of drums under this dome to-night will reverberate our reverent and grateful sympathy to the Empire's farthest bound. This memorable act of stoutest service gives response already to the rallying call of the poet-bishop of Australia:

> By all that have died for men,
>   By Christ who endured the Cross,
> Count nothing but honour gain,
>   Count all that is selfish loss.
>
> Take up with a loyal heart
>   The burden upon you laid;
> Who fights on the side of God
>   Needs never be afraid.
>
> Be true to the great good land,
>   And rear 'neath the Southern sun
> A race that shall hold its own,
>   And last till the world be done.[1]

"When in conditions the hardest and the most unpromising, Australia and New Zealand came successively to the birth a century ago, as a living part of the British Empire, who would have dared to fashion in remotest vision the stern, yet romantic, story of 1915? The eager manhood of the young raw Commonwealth, the product of our own time, first carried with swift safety across the successive seas, then disciplined and prepared for action under the shadow of the world-old Pyramids, and then gaining their first experience of the shock of the onset within sight and hearing of the plains of Troy —an almost inconceivable intermingling of the old world and the new. The bare story is itself a stimulus

[1] *Australia*, by Dr. Gilbert White, Bishop of Carpentaria.

and a reminder of what the lessons of history and the trust of Empire mean.

"God give us grace so to bear ourselves as a united people that we may be building out of this welter of fearful pain and strife the walls of His greater kingdom upon earth, the kingdom that is to endure : when the nations of the earth, and not least our own peoples—Britain and Canada and Australia and New Zealand and South Africa and India—bring into it, each of them, their honour and their glory, the distinctive powers and blessings that God has given to each several one, to make glad the city of our God, the habitation of the Prince of Peace."

At the conclusion of the Archbishop's sermon the band of the Guards played the Dead March in "Saul"; the bugles rang out in the "Last Post," and the mourners reverently left the building. So London paid its tribute to Australasia's dead.

THE ARMIES OF AUSTRALASIA

CHAPTER XV

THE ARMIES OF AUSTRALASIA

UNTIL the year 1870, the Imperial Government maintained a small body of troops in Australia for the defence of the country. They existed for two purposes: the chief one being to protect the country from risings of the convicts. The other purpose was to assist in repelling any foreign invasion, for they formed the garrisons of the rather primitive forts which protected some of the Australian harbours. From time to time local defence bodies were formed, when the troubles of the Mother Country seemed to bring a foreign invasion among the actual possibilities of Australian history. As soon as the trouble, whatever it might be, had blown over, these defence organizations would die a natural death, to be revived when fresh clouds appeared upon the horizon.

The withdrawal of the Imperial troops in 1870 forced each Australian state to initiate measures for defence, and caused the establishment of a small professional army in each of the six separate states, that were later federated into the Commonwealth of Australia. These very small groups of soldiers were designed to form a nucleus for a citizen defence force. This was purely voluntary, the men of Australia drilling and training without any payment; and the Governments finding uniform and weapons, and allowing a fairly large supply of ammunition for practice, at a very cheap rate.

In 1880 a militia system was substituted for the volunteer system, and a yearly payment of something like £12 for each volunteer soldier was arranged. At the same time an admirable cadet system was established, and the schoolboys of Australia entered into the business of drilling, training and shooting with an enthusiasm that did much to keep the ranks of the militia full, as they grew up. The smaller country settlements also established rifle clubs, which had a remarkably large membership. A little drill was combined with a great deal of shooting under service conditions, and to the rifle clubs Australia owes the possession of a very large number of sharpshooters that certainly have no superiors in the world.

The cadets attracted the notice of King George when, as Duke of York, he made his great Empire tour in 1900. They took part in a remarkable review of defence forces held on the famous Flemington racecourse; and Mr. E. F. Knight, one of the London journalists who accompanied the King on that tour, wrote of them in the following terms :—

"The first to pass the saluting base were the cadets, who to the stirring strains of the British Grenadiers marched by with a fine swing and preserved an excellent alignment. They presented the appearance of very tough young soldiers, and they exhibited no fatigue after a very trying day, in the course of which they had been standing for hours with soaked clothes in the heavy rain. They looked business-like in their khaki uniforms and felt hats.

"During the march past I was in a pavilion reserved chiefly for British and foreign naval officers. The German and American officers were much struck with the physique and soldierly qualities of the Australian troops, but they spoke with unreserved admiration when they saw these cadets."

The cadet system was elaborated, between the years 1909 and 1911, into a system of compulsory military training based on a scheme drawn up by Lord Kitchener himself, followed by a report on Australian defences made by Sir Ian Hamilton, the General who is now in supreme charge of the Australasian forces at the Dardanelles. When the new scheme came into force, the numbers of the land forces of the Commonwealth were nearly 110,000 men and boys; the figures comprising

2,000 permanent troops, nearly 22,000 militia, over 55,000 members of rifle clubs, and 28,000 cadets.

At the time the new compulsory system came into force, the number of males in Australia was—

Between 12 and 18 (of cadet age) . 260,000
Between 18 and 26 (of citizen soldier
    age) 366,000
Between 26 and 35 330,000
Between 35 and 60 614,000

For compulsory training it was enacted that the citizens of cadet and military age should be divided into four classes as under :—

Junior Cadets, from 12 to 14.
Senior Cadets, from 14 to 18.
Citizen soldiers, from 18 to 25.
       ,,   ,, 25 to 26.

The prescribed training was : (a) For junior cadets, 120 hours yearly. (b) For senior cadets, 4 whole-day drills, 12 half-day drills, and 24 night drills yearly. (c) For citizen soldiers, 16 whole-day drills, or their equivalent, of which not less than eight should be in camps of continuous training.

The scheme came into operation at the beginning of 1911, when the new cadets, to the number of over 120,000, were enrolled. At the same time 200 non-commissioned officers, as a training force

IN THE GREAT WAR 217

or the new army, went into camp for a six months course of instruction. From July 1 the new system of cadet training began, 20,000 of the boys, of the age of eighteen, going into training as the first year's crop of recruits. Every year afterwards this number, approximately, of trained senior cadets was added to the citizen army in training, while the number of cadets remained about 120,000; some 20,000 junior cadets at the age of twelve reinforcing the cadets as each draft of eighteen-year-old cadets became citizen soldiers.

It will be seen that the outbreak of the war in 1914 found the Australian scheme still incomplete, since the number of citizen soldiers in training was approximately only 80,000, even including the 20,000 cadets of that year, who had just been drafted into the citizen army.

Australia had also arranged for the training of its own young officers, who in time should develop into Area Officers under the compulsory services scheme, which provides for the division of the Commonwealth into over 200 military Areas, with an officer in charge of each. The establishment of a military college at Duntroon, near the new Australian Federal capital city of Canberra, had made excellent progress when war came.

The Duntroon establishment was an efficient rather than a showy establishment; its modest wooden bungalows, in which the officers were quartered, contrasting strangely with the elaborate arrangements at similar establishments such as Sandhurst or West Point. But the teaching was remarkably thorough for such a young institution. The democratic tendencies of Australia are illustrated by the fact that tuition at Duntroon is absolutely free, the parents of the young officer being not even asked to supply him with pocket money, since an allowance of 5s. per week is made by the Government to each cadet in training. The course of instruction is one of four years' training, and necessitates the daily application of six hours to instruction, and two hours to military exercises. A vacation of two months is observed at Christmas time, the height of the Australian summer, and there are frequent camps for practical instruction in all branches of field work.

Cadets are required to make their own beds, clean their own boots, and keep their kit in order. Special emphasis is laid upon the value of character, and any cadet, however able in acquiring knowledge or brilliant in physical exercises, must, if he lacks the power of self-discipline, be removed as unfit to become an officer who has to control others. The College was opened in June, 1911, with forty-one cadets, and has since been employed by the New Zealand Government for the training of its young officers, a step in co-operation which is likely to show the way to still closer relations

IN THE GREAT WAR 219

between the Dominion and the Commonwealth in many matters relating to defence.

The Commandant of the College was the late General Bridges, whose death in action at Gaba Tepe is so universally mourned by Australians. Writing of him and the College in the *Sydney Morning Herald*, V. J. M. says :—

"Duntroon is his masterpiece. To have left it as he did, after a bare four years, represents the greatest educational feat yet accomplished in Australia. Before attempting it he studied the greatest colleges in Europe and America— Sandhurst, Woolwich, West Point, Kingston, Saint-Cyr, L'Ecole Polytechnique, L'Ecole Militaire, die Grosslichterfelder Kadettenanstalt—all were visited and carefully investigated by him. His endeavour was to incorporate, so far as local conditions would allow, the best of each in Duntroon. How far he has succeeded is well known. In the opinion of Viscount Bryce, Sir Ian Hamilton, Sir Ronald Munro-Ferguson, and others, it stands out one of the most efficient military schools— some say the most efficient—in the world. Four years ago there were a station homestead and a rolling sweep of lonely country. What a strong driving force must have been behind it all. The crisis found Duntroon ready. Already seventy-one officers from its class-rooms and training fields are at the front, of whom some twenty have fallen. So excellent has been the work of these young soldiers in the desert camp that, in a recent letter, General Bridges mentioned that General Birdwood has specially written of them to the King. Australia will have reason in the troublous years ahead to be thankful that her great military school was conceived by a man of broad grasp and wide knowledge. The soldiers of the future will be moulded and the armies of the future organized by its graduates. He meant it to be, and it is, a great military university."

The precedent that Australasian soldiers should take part in the wars of the Mother Country was set in 1883, when the State of New South Wales sent a contingent of 800 infantry and artillery to the Soudan. The initiative in this matter was due to Mr. W. B. Dalley, then Premier of New South Wales. The force, after being reviewed by Lord Loftus, the State Governor, sailed from Sydney on March 3, 1883, on the transports *Iberia* and *Australasian*. The services rendered by them were comparatively slight; indeed, they were treated by the Imperial authorities as rather a gratuitous nuisance, intruding where their presence was not required. But the precedent had been set, and was followed by all the Dominions Overseas, on the outbreak of the African war.

Once again the War Office was inclined to regard the Greater Britons as useless interlopers, and the offer to provide cavalry was met with the historical cable that in Africa "foot soldiers only" were required. It is further a matter of history that the authorities very sensibly revised this estimate as the war progressed, and were glad of the services of every man who could ride and shoot. Contingent after contingent was despatched from Australasia, New Zealand especially providing a wealth of fine soldiers. In proportion to population, the Dominion supplied more men to fight the Empire's battle in South Africa than any part of the British realm.

CLEARING THE PACIFIC

CHAPTER XVI

CLEARING THE PACIFIC

WHEN the war broke out, the ports of Australasia lay within striking distance of German harbours, where lay a powerful squadron of armoured and light cruisers. A very real danger to Australasian shipping and seaports had to be encountered; and the first warlike steps taken by Australia and New Zealand were expeditions against Germany's Pacific Colonies.

At that time they were very considerable possessions, about 100,000 square miles in extent. Chief among them was Kaiser Wilhelm's Land, or, to give it its British appellation, German New Guinea, contiguous to the Australian possession of Papua, and 70,000 square miles in area. Next came the Bismarck Archipelago, better known as New Britain, a group of islands with an area of 20,000 square miles. Other colonies were German Samoa, and the Caroline, Marshall, Ladrone, Pelew, and Solomon Islands. In these colonies were established wireless stations of great strategical importance to Germany.

The squadron maintained to protect these possessions was a very modern and powerful one, as Great Britain was to learn to her cost. It consisted of the armoured cruisers *Scharnhorst* and *Gneisenau*, and the light fast cruisers *Leipzig*, *Nürnberg*, and *Emden*. The units of the British navy on the spot were the three old third-class cruisers *Psyche*, *Pyramus*, and *Philomel*; and upon these New Zealand, the Dominion most threatened, would have been forced to rely if Australia had not been provided with a navy of her own.

That navy had made ready for sea at the first sign of a great European war, and met at an appointed rendezvous off the coast of Queensland on August 11. One section of it, consisting of the battle-cruiser *Australia*, the light cruisers *Sydney* and *Melbourne*, and the destroyers *Parramatta*, *Yarra*, and *Warrego*, set off to the Bismarcks in the hope of encountering the German squadron. The destroyers, under convoy of the *Sydney*, made straight for Rabaul, the chief German settlement there, although there were no charts of the harbour, while the big ship and the other light cruiser kept watch at a distance.

In the darkness of a pitch-black night the destroyers steamed into the harbour, and captured all the ships in the bay. Right up to the pier they steamed, and then out again, having effected their purpose for the time being. They set out from that point to a rendezvous at Port Moresby, in Australian New Guinea, while the *Sydney* returned to Australian waters. The *Australia* and the *Melbourne* made for New Caledonia, where their presence was needed in aid of the Sister Dominion of New Zealand.

With the greatest secrecy the New Zealand Government had equipped a force of 1,300 volunteers from the province of Wellington, for an expedition against German Samoa. They knew the big German warships were somewhere in the vicinity, but that risk did not deter them. The men were sent on transports, and convoyed by one of the antiquated British cruisers; their first port of call was New Caledonia, distant five days. Fortune favours the brave, and this was a brave little adventure, if ever there were one such. But they won out all right, reaching New Caledonia safely, to receive a joyous welcome from the *Australia*, the *Melbourne*, and the French cruiser *Montcalm*, which were awaiting them at Noumea.

Their course to Samoa was now a safe one, comparatively speaking, and they had the satisfaction of lowering the German flag at Apia, and hoisting the Union Jack in its place, before the war was a month old. The warships left the

Expedition in possession, and steamed away. A fortnight later the two big German ships were sighted off the harbour, and the little garrison had a thrilling experience. They prepared to defend the place against the heavy guns of the Germans, but it was not necessary. After some delay the Germans, apparently fearing some trap, steamed off, and were not again seen in the vicinity.

Samoa fell on August 29, and on September 9 the *Australia* and the *Melbourne* were keeping another rendezvous at Port Moresby. Their appointment was with the transport *Berrima*, which, escorted by the cruiser *Sydney*, conveyed to that port an Expedition launched against the German Colonies in the North Pacific. It consisted of six companies of the Royal Australian Naval Reserve, under Colonel Holmes, D.S.O., and a battalion of infantry with machine guns. With the *Berrima* were the two Australian submarines AE1 and AE2, both of which came to an untimely end before the war was nine months old. At the rendezvous were the destroyers, a transport with 500 Queensland soldiers, and store ships and other requisites for such an expedition.

The objects of the expedition were two; they meant to occupy Rabaul, the chief settlement in the Bismarck Archipelago, and to destroy the German wireless station they knew to be established somewhere in Neu Pommern, the principal

The Australian Submarines AE 1 and AE 2, both lost in the First Year of War.

island in the group. The *Australia*, with the transports, made straight for Rabaul, which capitulated. The destroyers, under convoy of the *Sydney*, were sent forward to search for the wireless station. The first landing party marched straight inland, and soon encountered trouble. A heavy fire was directed upon them from sharpshooters, who were so well hidden that it was suspected they were in the trees; and the Australians were forced to take to the bush. They signalled for help, and also worked through the dense scrub until they came upon an entrenched position.

The signal for help brought every available man from the destroyers ashore; a picturesque touch was added to the reinforcement by the uninvited presence of one of the ship's butchers, who attached himself to the party in a blue apron, and armed with his cleaver of office. This relief party was followed by two others, one landing at Herbertshöhe to execute a flank movement. The first party had some stiff bush fighting, in which Lieutenant Bowen was wounded, and three Germans were captured. When the first two forces joined hands, Lieutenant-Commander Elwell was shot dead; and they were glad to see the main expeditionary force, with machine guns, arrive on the scene of action.

The machine guns settled the question, and the German commander, Lieutenant Kempf, at once hoisted the white flag. With some Australians he proceeded to a second line of trenches, and ordered the occupants to surrender. A number of them were taken prisoners; and then resistance broke out, and they all tried to escape. They were fired upon, and eighteen were shot in the act of running away. In the end the remainder were content to surrender.

The surrender of the wireless station was negotiated by Lieutenant Kempf himself, after giving his parole. He cycled alone to the place, and announced that he had arranged that there should be no resistance. Three Australian officers followed him and, placing reliance upon his word, boldly entered the station late at night. They found it strongly entrenched, but the natives who formed the majority of the defending force had quite understood Admiral Patey's threat that he would shell the place unless the flag were hauled down, and had no relish for such an ordeal. The next afternoon the British flag was hoisted over the station.

The next objective was Toma, a town inland whither the German administrator of the Colony had fled when the warships appeared before Rabaul. An expedition against this place, with the complement of a 12-pounder gun, was accordingly arranged. The *Australia* paved the way for this expedition by shelling the approaches to the town,

Rear-Admiral Sir George Patey,
commanding the Australian Squadron.

with the result that a deputation was sent out by the Administrator to meet the force half-way. The column continued its march without paying any attention to this deputation, and entered Toma the same day in a dense cloud of tropical rain.

The Administrator sent another messenger to the officer in charge, promising to repair to Herbertshöhe the next day to negotiate a surrender. As the French cruiser *Montcalm* had now arrived the most sanguine German could not expect any continued resistance, and the surrender was signed.

Thus on September 13 all resistance had been crushed in the Bismarck Islands, and the Colony had been reduced by the Australians at a cost of two officers killed—Captain Pockley and Lieutenant-Commander Elwell—and three men. One officer, Lieutenant Bowen, and three men were wounded.

On September 24 the warships put in an appearance at Friedrich Wilhelmshafen, the chief settlement in German New Guinea, where no resistance was encountered. That evening the German flag was blotted out of the Pacific Ocean, the last of the German colonies there having fallen to the energetic Australian navy.

Two wireless stations established by the Germans, one at Nauru and the other at Anguar, were seized and destroyed, to the disadvantage of the German Pacific squadron, against which the Australian navy now directed its operations, taking a prominent part in the driving movement which finally committed them to the battle of the Falkland Islands and their destruction by Admiral Sturdee on December 8.

THE YOUNGEST NAVY IN THE WORLD

CHAPTER XVII

THE YOUNGEST NAVY IN THE WORLD

ON the morning when the news of the sinking of the *Emden* reached London there was at least one good Briton of that city whose elation was curiously mingled with puzzlement. He was puzzled to know how Australia came by a navy; he had seen references to an Australian navy before, but had always supposed that a misprint had been made for "Austrian navy."

His wonder is so far excusable that the first ship of that navy was only launched as recently as 1911, when the battle cruiser *Australia* left the stocks in the yards of Messrs. John Brown & Co., of Glasgow; and she only arrived in Australia two years later. The other units of the navy are of even later construction. The existence of these vessels in Australian waters is a tribute to the enterprise and foresight of the Commonwealth of Australia. Their history and performance since the outbreak of the war has utterly confounded the naval experts of this country, who, if they had

had their way, would not have had such ships in such a place.

For a quarter of a century before the foundation of the Australian navy, the whole question of naval protection for Australasia had been one profoundly unsatisfactory, both to the Imperial government and to the governments of the Southern Nations. Australia and New Zealand paid a naval subsidy to the Imperial coffers; recently it amounted to the annual sum of £200,000 from Australia and £40,000 from New Zealand. In return, the Admiralty maintained a number of obsolete warcraft in Australian waters, at a cost vastly exceeding the annual tribute. The Australasians wanted better ships; the Imperial Government desired a larger subsidy; it was an arrangement that pleased nobody.

The makeshift fleet in Australasian waters was explained by postulating the theory that when trouble came, the battle for the defence of Australasia would be fought in the North Sea, or somewhere far from the reach of Australasian ports. The experience of the first twelve months of the war may surely be held to have exploded that theory. The North Sea fleet did not prevent the *Emden* from bombarding Madras, and sinking merchant shipping worth £2,500,000 in Eastern waters. It would not have prevented the *Scharnhorst* and *Gneisenau* from battering Wellington and Sydney,

IN THE GREAT WAR 237

and destroying half the ships in Australasian waters. But the theory was the pet one of all the experts, and it was employed seriously to disturb the pleasant relations between the Motherland and the Dominions.

For, about the year 1905, the uncontestable fact that the Dominions were not contributing sufficiently to the naval protection of the Empire could no longer be evaded. The question was discussed at Colonial Conferences ; it was the subject of bitter newspaper articles. The Dominions wished to meet some part, at least, of their great obligations, but not in the way required by the Imperial Government. Put bluntly, the demand made of them was tribute ; they were to supply money for naval defence, and have no voice in its expenditure.

Canada took a straightforward course, and withdrew her naval subsidy. New Zealand, with an admirable spirit, had a Dreadnought built, and handed it over to the Imperial Government. The battle cruiser *New Zealand* has done fine service in the North Sea since the outbreak of war, but had Australia been as sentimentally generous, Australasia would certainly have had cause to regret it.

But Australia planned to build a navy of her own ; and a scheme for the construction of the first instalment of warships was drawn up by Commander

Cresswell, now first naval adviser to the Commonwealth. He came to London in 1906 to support his scheme, and to his sane and able advocacy of it Australia and the Empire owe a debt it will be hard to repay. It would be possible to quote some of the criticism he received here, but it would serve no good end. Suffice to say, it was couched in the superior vein that proves so irritating to the Colonial in Great Britain, especially when he knows he is right.

At the Colonial Conference of 1907, the matter came up for discussion, and Mr. Deakin and Senator Pearce, who represented Australia, succeeded in carrying their point. Expert reports were obtained, the probable cost was reckoned, and bravely faced; and Australia began to build her own warships. It is an open secret that she did so with the tacit disapproval of the Admiralty, and in face of the violent criticism of the experts.

Thus it happened that when war broke out, the Australians were able to place at the disposal of the Admiralty the following up-to-date warships in Australasian waters :—

The battle cruiser *Australia* of 19,200 tons displacement, in length 555 feet, with an 80 foot beam, and a draught of $26\frac{1}{2}$ feet. Her armament consists of eight 12-inch guns, sixteen 4-inch guns, and two torpedo tubes. Of her ship's company of 820 more than half are Australians. She flies

H.M.A.S. "Australia" in Sydney Harbour.

the flag of Rear-Admiral Sir George Patey, K.C.V.O.

Three light cruisers: the *Sydney, Melbourne,* and *Brisbane,* all of 5,600 tons displacement, and with a speed of 26 knots. (The *Sydney* made 27 when steaming to her duel with the *Emden.*) Each has eight 6-inch guns, four 3-pounders, four machine guns and two torpedo tubes. The *Sydney* and *Melbourne* were built in Great Britain, but the *Brisbane* is of local construction.

Six destroyers: the *Parramatta, Yarra, Torrens, Warrego, Swan,* and *Derwent.* All are of the same type; of 700 tons displacement, 26 knots speed, and carry one 4-inch gun, three 12-pounders and three torpedo tubes.

Two submarines: the AE1 and AE2.

Thus had Australia provided for the defence of her coast, at a cost which excited strenuous criticism in the Commonwealth itself. Until war broke out—then every penny of the money was saved by the 12-inch guns of the *Australia.* " No," wrote an officer of the *Scharnhorst,* shortly before Admiral Sturdee had made an end of that armoured cruiser, " we did not raid any Australian port, nor sink any Australasian shipping. And why? Because we knew our 8·2-inch guns were no match for the armament of the *Australia.*"

It is instructive to contrast the events in Eastern waters, where the Admiralty, in pursuance of the great theory that the Empire was to be saved by a battle in the North Sea, had weakened the China fleet almost in proportion to the strength supplied in Southern waters on Australian initiative. The operations against Kiao-Chau so far occupied the British warships that the *Emden* was able to bombard Bombay, to enter the British port at Singapore and to sink the warships of our Allies while at anchor under the protection of the Empire's flag, and to heap insult and damage upon the first sea power of the world.

New Zealand, but for the Australian fleet, would have been as defenceless as the East Indies. The Dominion, while thrilled with a genuine and comprehensible pride at the fine work done elsewhere by its Dreadnought, was frank in admitting that the practical end of the argument lay with Australia. Mr. Massey, the Prime Minister, in a speech of the utmost import to Australasia, declared that the future policy of the Dominion would be one of co-operation with the Commonwealth for the naval defence of Australasian shores.

The work of the Australian warships in the reduction of the German Pacific Colonies has already been detailed. In the first seven weeks of the war the *Australia* and the *Melbourne* covered 12,000 miles. Not a single British merchant ship was molested in Australasian waters, while all the German shipping in the locality was gobbled up in the most summary fashion. Then, their work at home being completed, the vessels of the Australian fleet set out for wider adventures.

Some day the manœuvres which led to the destruction of the German Pacific squadron will be described by an expert, and the world will know what part the *Australia* played in bringing about that desired consummation. A cruise of 48,000 miles, by which the marauders were swept ever farther East, was the share of the battle cruiser of the Commonwealth. She burned 5,000 tons of coal and 6,000 tons of oil fuel, and had the satisfaction of overhauling and sinking a big German liner, of the Woermann line, which was fitted as a store ship and laden with all sorts of necessaries for the German warships. Later she was visible at a British port, where, after an official inspection, Admiral Patey was complimented on the fact that her guns were still in better order than those of any vessel of his Majesty's fleets. She is now serving the Empire many thousands of miles from her own waters, and when next the *New Zealand* is heard of, it may well be that the *Australia* also will be there.

The *Melbourne* and the *Sydney* returned, somewhat unwillingly, to undertake that convoy work which, incidentally, resulted so disastrously for the *Emden*. The present outlook promises that much will still be found for them to do in this direction, for the passage of Australasian troops through the Indian Ocean has now been regularized, and the supply is in course of being enormously increased.

The fate of Submarine AE1 was later shared by AE2, in a bold attempt to enter the Sea of Marmora, having pierced the Dardanelles as far as the Narrows. AE2 possessed, it is claimed, the record for a submarine in distance covered, for her operations during the war extended over a distance of 30,000 miles. Before misfortune overtook her, she had rendered excellent service at the Dardanelles. Her officers, and all her crew save nine, fell into the hands of the Turks, and are now in Turkish prisons.

Such has been the performance in twelve months of the vessels which form the nucleus of a fleet which will one day consist of fifty-two vessels and be manned by 15,000 men. It is intended by Australia that the warships shall be manned and officered by Australians, and with that end in view, training establishments for navel cadets and for sailors have been established in the Commonwealth. The Australian Naval College is still in its infancy, but it occupies a magnificent position at Jervis Bay, about eighty miles south of Sydney, on the coast of New South Wales.

An area of nearly fifteen square miles has been reserved for the establishment, and modest buildings have already been erected for the future Australian middies. A fine stream flows into the bay, and bathing and boating facilities are admirable. The College was occupied in March, 1915, and a start was made with twenty-four boys of thirteen years of age, selected from a large number of applications. The quality of the boys is illustrated by an incident of the first few months.

One youngster, during a game of cricket, was injured so seriously by the ball that an operation was immediately necessary. The lad walked into surgery, and saluted the doctor, who informed him that an anæsthetic would be necessary. The boy drew himself up proudly. " For the credit of the the service, sir," he said, " I must decline."

This naval college—the only one in the Dominions —will in 1916 have 150 picked lads in training.

The Royal Australian College is open to all classes. In the first quota of Cadet Midshipmen— it should be noted that in Australia the English term " Naval Cadet " has a different meaning— more than one half were pupils of State Schools. The cadets enter the College at the age of thirteen and from that day all their expenses are borne by the Commonwealth Government, even to the munificent grant of one shilling a week in pocket money. In return the boy is required to remain in the navy for a period of twelve years on attaining the age of eighteen, that is, on completing a four-year course at the College. A penalty of £75 for each year's training undergone will be imposed on parents or guardians who withdraw a cadet midshipman without the consent of the Australian Naval Board.

Appointments to the College are made by the Minister for Defence, upon the recommendation of the Naval Board, from such candidates as are considered suitable by the Selection Committee, and who have afterwards passed a qualifying examination in educational subjects. Nominations bearing a certain proportion to the number of midshipmen required for the College in any particular entry are allotted by the Governor-General in Council, as nearly as possible in the following proportions :— New South Wales, 38 per cent.; Victoria, 31 per cent.; Queensland, 12 per cent.; South Australia, 10 per cent.; Western Australia, 6 per cent.; Tasmania, 3 per cent.

For the selection of the most promising youths an interviewing committee, on properly advertised dates, sits at Brisbane, Sydney, Melbourne, Adelaide, and Hobart; Adelaide doing duty also for Western Australia, and Brisbane for the Northern Territory and Papua. The interviewing committee consists of the Captain of the College, Captain of Training Ship, District Naval Officer, Director of Education (with consent of the State Government), and a Naval Medical Officer.

On a similarly adequate basis, arrangements have been made for the instruction of sailors on training ships at several of the chief ports. The quality

The Governor-General of Australia

of the young Australian sailors on the *Australia* and the *Sydney* was one of the most satisfactory features of the fine service rendered by those vessels.

Such, in brief, are the main features of the scheme now in successful operation for the establishment of an adequate Australian Navy. What has been written above is written in no sense of useless recrimination or vainglorious boasting. The Dominions are asking for a conference with the Imperial authorities to discuss matters of Empire defence. One of the reasons which impels them to press for it now, and not hereafter, may be found in a conversation in which a leading citizen from Overseas voiced an opinion too little heard in Great Britain, but familiar enough to those who are in touch with Oversea ideals.

"You shout with rage," he said, "when some big German cruisers slip across the sea in the night and pump a few shells into a one-horse town like Scarborough. But when a little ashcat like the *Emden* holds up the proudest ports in your wide Empire, and gets off scot-free with her little 4-inch guns, you chuckle and say her captain is a fine sport. A conference is wanted to teach some of your big men a little Empire sense."

Perhaps there is something in that.

THE REWARD OF VALOUR

CHAPTER XVIII

THE REWARD OF VALOUR

BEFORE the Australians had been four weeks on Gallipoli, one of them at least had earned the Victoria Cross, on the great day when Sanders Pasha attempted to drive them into the sea. The award was gazetted on July 24, in the following terms :—

The Victoria Cross

No. 465 Lce.-Cpl. ALBERT JACKA, 14th Australian Imperial Forces. For most conspicuous bravery on the night of May 19-20, at "Courtney's Post," Gallipoli. While holding a portion of our trench with four other men he was heavily attacked. When all except himself were killed or wounded the trench was rushed and occupied by seven Turks, he at once most gallantly attacked them single-handed and killed the whole party, five by rifle fire and two with the bayonet.

In the *London Gazette* of July 2 appeared the first list of awards for bravery and distinguished service made to Australasians. The list is a long one, though it covers only in part the deeds of the first fortnight in Gallipoli. The following are the soldiers honoured by the King:—

AUSTRALIA

Distinguished Service Order

Lieut.-Colonel WALTER RAMSAY McNICOLL, 6th (Vic.) Battalion. On the night of April 25-26, 1915, during operations near Gaba Tepe, for repeatedly exhibiting great gallantry and skill in the command of his battalion.

Lieut.-Colonel CYRIL BRUDENELL BINGHAM WHITE, Royal Australian Garrison Artillery, Staff. During the operations near Gaba Tepe on April 25, 1915, and subsequently for his distinguished service co-ordinating staff work, and in re-organization after the inevitable dislocation and confusion arising from the first landing operations. He displayed exceptional ability.

Major CHARLES HENRY BRAND, 3rd Australian Infantry Brigade. On April 25, 1915, during operations in the neighbourhood of Gaba Tepe, for conspicuous gallantry and ability in organizing stragglers under heavy fire, and for organizing and leading an attack resulting in the disablement of three of the enemy's guns. Major Brand conveyed messages himself on many occasions under fire during emergencies.

Major JAMES SAMUEL DENTON, 11th (W.A.)

IN THE GREAT WAR 251

Battalion. During the operations in the neighbourhood of Gaba Tepe on April 25, 1915, for valuable services in obtaining and transmitting information to ships' guns and mountain batteries, and subsequently for holding a trench, with about twenty men, for over six days, repulsing several determined attacks.

Major JAMES HEANE, 4th (N.S.W.) Battalion. On May 1, 1915, during the operations near Gaba Tepe, for displaying conspicuous gallantry in leading his company to the support of a small force which, in an isolated trench, was without means of reinforcement, replenishment, or retreat. He attained his object at a heavy sacrifice.

Major WILLIAM OWEN MANSBRIDGE, 16th (S.A. and W.A.) Battalion. On April 25, 1915, during operations near Gaba Tepe, for exceptional gallantry and resource during the first assault, and again on May 2 and 3, during an assault on a difficult position.

Major ROBERT RANKINE, 14th (Vic.) Battalion. On the night of April 26-27, 1915, during operations in the neighbourhood of Gaba Tepe, for gallantly leading an assault resulting in the capture of a most important post, and subsequently for holding that position against repeated attacks for five days without relief.

Capt. ARTHUR GRAHAM BUTLER, Australian Army Medical Corps (attached 9th (Q.) Battalion).

During operations in the neighbourhood of Gaba Tepe on April 25, 1915, and subsequent dates, for conspicuous gallantry and devotion to duty in attending wounded under heavy fire, continuously displaying courage of a high order.

Military Cross

Capt. JASPER KENNETH GORDON MAGEE, 4th (N.S.W.) Battalion. On April 25, 1915, and subsequent dates, during operations in the neighbourhood of Gaba Tepe, for gallantry in leading his men, and exhibiting sound judgment and ability on several occasions, under a constant and harassing fire.

Capt. CLIFFORD RUSSELL RICHARDSON, 2nd (N.S.W.) Battalion. On April 25, 1915, during operations near Gaba Tepe, for displaying great coolness and courage, and leading a charge against superior numbers under a heavy cross-fire, resulting in the flight of the enemy in disorder.

Capt. JAMES WILLIAM ALBERT SIMPSON, 13th (N.S.W.) Battalion. On May 2, 1915, during an attack in the neighbourhood of Gaba Tepe, for showing conspicuous bravery and skill in directing the battalion through unreconnoitred scrub. He was conspicuously active in consolidating the position gained under heavy fire.

Lieut. ALFRED PLUMLEY DERHAM, 5th (Vic.) Battalion. On April 25, 1915, and subsequently

Captain Richardson of the 1st Brigade, who was awarded the Military Cross for his fine work at the landing.

during operations in the neighbourhood of Gaba Tepe, for acting with great bravery and ability, and continuing to do duty until April 30, although shot through the thigh on April 25.

Lieut. CHARLES FORTESCUE, 9th (Q.) Battalion. From April 25 to 29, 1915, during operations near Gaba Tepe, for conspicuous gallantry. He twice led charges against the enemy, and rendered good service in collecting reinforcements and organizing stragglers.

Lieut. REGINALD GEORGE LEGGE, 13th (N.S.W.) Battalion. On May 1 and 2, 1915, during operations in the neighbourhood of Gaba Tepe, for conspicuous ability and courage in the successful handling of his machine-gun section. On several occasions he inflicted severe losses on the enemy, and was himself severely wounded in the neck.

Lieut. ALFRED JOHN SHOUT, 1st (N.S.W.) Battalion. On April 27, 1915, during operations near Gaba Tepe for showing conspicuous courage and ability in organizing and leading his men in a thick, bushy country, under very heavy fire. He frequently had to expose himself to locate the enemy, and led a bayonet charge at a critical moment.

No. 96 Sgt.-Maj. D. SMITH, 5th (Vic.) Battalion. On May 8, 1915, during operations south of Krithia, for conspicuous gallantry and good services in rallying and leading men forward to the attack.

254 GLORIOUS DEEDS OF AUSTRALASIANS

Although wounded in both arms, he continued to direct his men, setting a valuable example of devotion to duty.

Distinguished Conduct Medal

No. 6 Sgt. A. ANDERSON, 2nd (N.S.W.) Battalion. For conspicuous gallantry on April 25, 1915, and subsequent dates, during the operations near Gaba Tepe, in assisting to reorganize small parties of various battalions under heavy fire and placing them in the firing line.

No. 189 Sgt. W. AYLING, 11th (W.A.) Battalion. On April 15, 1915, during operations near Gaba Tepe, for gallantry in commanding his platoon after his officer had been wounded. When compelled to retire he carried the wounded officer with him, and on obtaining reinforcements again led his platoon to the attack.

No. 695 Pte. W. J. BIRRELL, C Co., 7th (Vic.) Battalion. On May 8, 1915, during operations near Krithia, for distinguished conduct in collecting and organizing men who had become detached, and leading them to a weak flank of the firing line.

No. 170 L.-Cpl. P. BLACK, 16th (S.A. and W.A.) Battalion. On the night of May 2-3, 1915, during operations near Gaba Tepe, for exceptional gallantry. After all his comrades in the machine-gun section had been killed or wounded, and although surrounded by the enemy, he fired all available ammunition, and finally brought his gun out of action.

No. 997 Pte. L. W. BURNETT, Australian A.M.C. From April 25 to May 5, 1915, during operations near Gaba Tepe, for exceptionally gallant work and devotion to duty under heavy fire.

No. 182 Sgt. W. A. CONNELL, 12th (S.A., W.A. and Tas.) Battalion. On April 25, 1915, during operations near Gaba Tepe, for gallantly attacking an entrenched position and an enemy's machine gun.

No. 94 Staff Sgt-Maj. M. E. E. CORBETT, 15th (Q. and Tas.) Battalion. On May 3, 1915, during operations near Gaba Tepe, for exceptional gallantry in serving his machine gun after he had been wounded, until it was put out of action, and again for rallying men and leading them to a second attack, retrieving a difficult situation.

Driver G. DEAN, Australian Div. Sig. Co. On May 8, 1915, during operations near Krithia, for distinguished gallantry. Was detailed to accompany four officers to the firing line to lay telephone wire. Owing to the heavy fire only one officer reached the position. Driver Dean kept up constant communication with brigade headquarters until 3 a.m. on May 9, when the remaining officer was wounded. Alone, he assisted this officer back and attended other wounded men, but never neglected his duties on the telephone.

No. 325 Pte. A. FARMER, 3rd (N.S.W.) Battalion. On April 25, 1915, during operations near Gaba Tepe, for gallantry in repeatedly carrying messages and twice going back for ammunition under severe rifle and machine-gun fire ; and again, on April 27, when his officer was wounded, for organizing a party of three men who carried the wounded officer to the rear. Private Farmer exposed himself fearlessly, and it was owing to his coolness and initiative that the party succeeded. He was himself wounded.

No. 851 L.-Cpl. W. FRANCIS, 13th (N.S.W.) Battalion. On May 3, 1915, during operations near Gaba Tepe, for great bravery in removing wounded from the trenches to a dressing station over ground swept by machine-gun fire.

No. 764 L.-Cpl. H. W. FREAME, 1st (N.S.W.) Battalion. On April 25, 1915, and subsequently during the operations near Gaba Tepe, for displaying the utmost gallantry in taking water to the firing line although twice hit by snipers.

No. 918 Pte. F. GODFREY, 12th (S.A., W.A. and Tas.) Battalion. On April 25, 1915, during operations near Gaba Tepe, for exceptionally gallant conduct in personally capturing an enemy officer, and going out single-handed and shooting five enemy snipers.

No. 1293 Pte. R. HUMBERTSON, 3rd (N.S.W.) Battalion. On April 25, 1915, and subsequently during operations near Gaba Tepe, for conspicuous coolness and bravery in volunteering on many occasions for dangerous missions and for judgment in carrying them out.

Staff-Sgt. H. JACKSON, Australian A.M.C. From April 25 until May 5, 1915, during operations near Gaba Tepe, for exceptionally gallant work and devotion to duty under heavy fire.

No. 75 L.-Cpl. T. KENNEDY, 1st (N.S.W.) Battalion. On April 25, 1915, and subsequent dates, during operations near Gaba Tepe, for displaying the greatest coolness and pluck in running round under heavy fire and collecting stragglers, whom he formed and led into the firing line. This he did time after time, with excellent results.

No. 741 L.-Cpl. J. KENYON, 9th (Q.) Battalion. On April 25, 1915, during operations near Gaba Tepe, for conspicuous courage and initiative in returning from the firing line under heavy fire, collecting reinforcements, and assisting in leading a successful bayonet charge to the top of a hill, which was eventually held against great odds.

No. 99 Spr. G. F. MCKENZIE, 3rd Field Co., Australian Engineers. On May 4, 1915, during a landing and an attack on the enemy's redoubt near Gaba Tepe, for conspicuous gallantry in rescuing a wounded sapper and carrying him back to the boat under heavy fire. Having pushed the boat off, he himself returned to the beach, and was subsequently wounded.

No. 280 Pte. A. C. B. MERRIN, 5th (Vic.) Battalion. On April 25, 1915, and subsequently during operations on the Gallipoli Peninsula, for exhibiting on many occasions the greatest courage and coolness in carrying messages, helping wounded, and bringing up food and water under heavy fire.

No. 115 L.-Cpl. R. I. MOORE, 3rd (N.S.W.) Battalion. From April 25 until April 29, 1915, during operations near Gaba Tepe. Commanded his section under heavy and continuous fire from snipers who were within thirty yards of his trench. He displayed exceptional courage in twice advancing alone about twenty yards, and on the second occasion he accounted for five of the enemy.

No. 530 Pte. G. ROBEY, 9th (Q.) Battalion. On April 25, 1915, during operations near Gaba Tepe, for conspicuous gallantry in swimming to a boat and bringing back into safety a wounded comrade who was the only occupant. This was done under heavy fire.

No. 1088 Cpl. E. ROBSON, 4th (N.S.W.) Battalion. On May 1, 1915, during operations near Gaba Tepe, for distinguished conduct in the command of a platoon, guiding and controlling the men after the officer commanding the platoon had been wounded. Although in an exposed position he personally carried up ammunition, and freely exposed himself.

No. 41 Staff Segt.-Maj. A. STEELE, 9th (Q.) Battalion. From April 25 to 29, 1915, during operations near Gaba Tepe, for distinguished conduct in manning and maintaining his machine gun, which he continued to work after the remainder of his section had been killed or wounded.

No. 791 Pte. W. UPTON, 13th (N.S.W.) Battalion. On April 25, 1915, during operations near Gaba Tepe, for great bravery in bringing wounded into shelter, and again on May 2, after being shot through the foot, in continuing to defend his trench until again wounded.

No. 456 Pte. J. C. WEATHERILL, 10th (S.A.) Battalion. On April 25, 1915, during operations near Gaba Tepe, for exceptionally good work in scouting and in an attack resulting in the capture of two of the enemy's guns.

No. 213 Pte. A. WRIGHT, 15th (Q. and Tas.) Battalion. On the night of May 2-3, 1915, during operations near Gaba Tepe, for repeated instances of gallantry when acting as a scout and guide to his unit.

NEW ZEALAND

Distinguished Service Order

Major HERBERT HART, Wellington Battalion 17th (Ruahine) Regiment. On April 26, 1915, during operations near Gaba Tepe, for distinguished service in rallying men and digging into an important forward position in the face of an extremely severe fire. The country was wooded and difficult, and unreconnoitred, and his force was subject to constant surprise attacks.

Major EUGENE JOSEPH O'NEILL, F.R.C.S., N.Z. Medical Corps. On April 25 and 26, 1915, during operations near Gaba Tepe, for exceptionally good service, and exhibiting initiative and resource in command of a bearer sub-division.

Major FREDERICK WAITE, N.Z. Engineers. On the night of May 2-3, 1915, during operations in the neighbourhood of Gaba Tepe, for gallantry and resource in rallying his men and leading them forward at critical moments.

Capt. ARTHUR CUNLIFFE BERNARD CRITCHLEY-SALMONSON, the Royal Munster Fusiliers (attached N.Z. Forces). During operations in the neighbourhood of Gaba Tepe on April 25, 1915, for great gallantry and resource in command of a small party, and saving a difficult situation. Again, on the night of May 2-3, he successfully led a small party to an advanced trench under great difficulties.

Military Cross

Capt. JESSE ALFRED WALLINGFORD, N.Z. Staff Corps. On April 25 and 26, 1915, during operations near Gaba Tepe, for exceptionally good services with the New Zealand Brigade machine gun and sharpshooters, and for conspicuous coolness and resource on several critical occasions.

No. 8/1048 Sgt.-Maj. A. W. PORTEOUS, 10th (North Otago) Regiment. On April 26, 1915, during operations in the neighbourhood of Gaba Tepe, for gallantry in action, and again on the night of May 2–3, for exceptional bravery and devotion to duty. All the officers of his company being killed or wounded, he organized and led the company, continually exposing himself for four hours, and showing fine military spirit and powers of leadership.

Distinguished Conduct Medal

No. 4/208A Cpl. C. W. SALMON, N.Z. Eng. On May 2, 1915, during operations near Gaba Tepe, and again on May 5, for conspicuous bravery in defending exposed portions of the position.

No. 4/60A Cpl. C. W. SAUNDERS, N.Z. Eng. On April 27, 1915, during operations near Gaba Tepe for gallantly leading part of his section to occupy a trench which had been vacated, and for exceptional zeal and intelligence in sapping operations.

No. 3/95 L.-Cpl. W. SINGLETON, N.Z. Field Ambulance. From April 25 until May 5, 1915, during operations near Gaba Tepe, for exceptionally gallant work and devotion to duty under heavy fire.

No. 3/447 L.-Cpl. G. STEEDMAN, N.Z. Medical Corps. On April 27, 1915, during operations near Gaba Tepe, for gallantly rescuing a wounded man under fire, and again on April 29, for attending on two wounded men under heavy fire.

No. 6/1156 Pte T. STOCKDILL, Stretcher Bearer, Canterbury Battalion. On April 26, 1915, during operations near Gaba Tepe, for distinguished gallantry in recovering wounded men on the open beach under heavy fire.

No. 10/1674 Pte. J. W. SWANN, Wellington Battalion. On May 2 and 3, 1915, during operations near Gaba Tepe, for distinguished service on three separate occasions in making valuable reconnaissances under heavy fire.

No. 12/1012 Pte. G. TEMPANY, Auckland Battalion. On May 25, 1915, during operations near Gaba Tepe, for conspicuous bravery during a retirement in advancing under heavy fire into the enemy's lines, and carrying back a wounded comrade into safety.

No. 1476 L.-Cpl. J. WIMMS, N.Z. Div. Train. On April 25 and 26, 1915, during operations near Gaba Tepe, for setting an example of gallantry and devotion to duty in distributing ammunition and water to the firing line under heavy fire.

THE AUSTRALASIAN SOLDIER

CHAPTER XIX

THE AUSTRALASIAN SOLDIER

And Southern Nation, and Southern State aroused from
their dream of ease,
Shall write in the book of Eternal Fate their stormy
histories.

"THE Australasians are possibly the finest troops in the world."

The considered judgment of an observer at the Dardanelles, Mr. Josiah Wedgwood, M.P., deliberately pronounced for publication in the Press, caught the attention of many readers of newspapers in this country. Cabled out to the Southern Hemisphere, it was reproduced in every newspaper in Australia and New Zealand, where a thrill of pride and gratitude vibrated from end to end of the country, radiating back to the most remote township at the very Back of Beyond.

This was generous appreciation indeed, and accepted in the same spirit of generosity in which it was tendered. The vow, "Our last shilling and our last man," with which Australasia had solemnly entered upon the Great War was as solemnly renewed. The Southern Britons quivered with comprehensible pride at the generous and timely praise; it was more than they would have claimed—much more—but it carried a message of consolation to many a stricken home ten thousand miles away from the blood-stained battlefields of Europe. "Good soldiers, none better!" Then they have not died for nothing if they have merited that epitaph from the Motherland.

Nature, as well as the deliberate plan of the Australasians themselves, has ensured that an army of Australasians must necessarily compose a very fine fighting force. It may be that the qualifications of the soldier of the future shall consist of an incredible callousness of heart, and an extended knowledge of all the detestable forms that can be assumed by the most hideous of human crimes. But the qualifications of a warrior have not yet been so far modified by the Great War that he has been converted into a poisoner. It is still assumed that he is a man who risks his life in the fair fight he wages with fair-minded men, whom unfortunate circumstances have made his foes for the time being. Coolness and resource in danger, magnanimity in the glory of victory, and stoutheartedness in the first abashment of defeat may still be called the soldier's virtues; and the oldest excuse for war, that the soldier

Farewell to the Troops in Melbourne.

kills without murder in his heart, can still be pleaded by the Briton who takes up arms in defence of his country.

Soldiering of this sort has always been an instinct with the Southern Briton. The individual citizen there is under no misapprehension about the preparedness of his country for war; he looks around and sees for himself. To desire to retain a great continent for ever for the exclusive use of the white races is a privilege involving heavy responsibilities. There is an obvious danger in excluding one's neighbours because they do not conform to the high ideals of civilization adopted by the Briton. Very deliberately the Australasian has adopted this provocative attitude toward his coloured neighbours, who far outnumber him, though possessing only very restricted areas of territory for their habitation, as compared with the spacious elbow room which the Australasian reserves for himself.

From his early boyhood the young Australasian is made familiar with the possibility of taking up arms in self-defence. Whatever may be thought of the measures he takes for the development of his holding, in proof of his title to it, there can be no difference of opinion as to his readiness to fight for his spacious heritage. He knows what such a war would mean to his country, with its long stretches of undefended coastline, and the sparse population of the country behind them. These coasts are so obviously vulnerable spots that only a purblind fool could ignore their terrible significance. And the Australasian is certainly no fool.

There are other circumstances, too, in his daily life that may be partly responsible for his curious readiness to take off his coat and fight. The uncertainty of his surroundings may be responsible for his belief that life is one long fight with circumstance. He goes forth to his daily occupation with the light of battle in his eye; there is something pathetically cynical in his creed that it is necessary to fight for what he gets, even after he has fairly earned it by more peaceful means. He gives his admiration to the man he calls a "battler," and reserves a contemptuous surprise for the man who expects to get anything at all without fighting for it.

Wherever he comes into contact with Nature, the Australasian finds justification for his idea that life is a long struggle against adverse conditions, a struggle which must only be relinquished at the merciful call of Death itself. Considering the fewness of his numbers, he is engaged in the most terrific task that engages any of the nations of the world. He is developing a vast unknown continent, and contending with conditions that are most curiously fickle. The unconsidered circumstances of one year become the determining factors of the next, and that by some whimsical no-law that baffles all intelligent prevision. In another century he may have mastered some of the tricks that climate and environment, to mention but two of his ever-present problems, are playing with his means of livelihood; for the present they make his existence one long uncertain struggle.

For instance, a bag of seed wheat brought from another district may contain a few seeds of a harmless weed, known for many years to be innocent; not worth worrying about one way or the other. The transfer to new conditions of soil and atmosphere suddenly transforms this inoffensive plant into a vegetable pest, that climbs over all saner growths and chokes them out of existence with the ineradicable monstrosity of its new functions. Fertile farms are rendered useless, and the product of the work of whole lifetimes negatived by such malevolent miracles; but they give the Australasian the fighting spirit. Two or three men will go out and face a roaring bush fire with a two-mile front, in the apparently hopeless task of holding it in check till further assistance can be procured. Drought, flood and pestilence are fought in the same uncompromising way, for the race has the instinct of grim battle implanted deep down in its nature. The Australasian knows there is always something to contend with; he knows it is no use to expect a soft time; he must fight.

So he becomes resourceful, inventive, open to suggestion. He is certain there is a counter to every blow delivered by Fate, if one could but discover it. To expect to fight, to realize that there is always a chance to win, but a reasonable expectation of defeat, to seek expedients without being discouraged by failure; all these things make good training for soldiering. They are all part of the daily life of the Australasian, even of the Australasian of the cities. Disaster, sudden and swift; change, inexorable and sweeping; disappointment, bitter and undeserved; he recognizes them all as everyday factors in his existence. The fighting spirit cannot be held long in abeyance if they are to be countered and overcome.

Then the Australasian has the fighting equipment. He is superbly healthy, in spite of his leanness and the drawn look due to the lines that life bites into the faces of even the young men. These men of the sun-dried plains and the rocky ranges look upon illness as something unnatural, something to be ashamed of and concealed; they seem almost to have the instinct that prompts the sick animal to hide from its fellows, and sometimes impels the hale beasts to slay the sick one for the reason that illness is unnatural, dangerous, and an offence. Australasia has the lowest death-rate of the world, a significant fact in the health record of a nation. A nation of athletes! Swift runners, fast swimmers, tall lean men whose movements are made with incredible and deceptive swiftness, inured to the saddle and to long marches under a tropical sun. Compare a regiment of them with a regiment of home-bred Britons, and the advantage in smartness of appearance would lie with the latter. The Australasian is inclined to be loose-jointed and slabby; they use the word "lanky" themselves. They are inclined to economy of physical effort, to walk with a slouch and a swing. Do not be misled by the lack of "snap" in their movements; it is deceptive.

Enterprise and daring are theirs by heredity. They have descended from a race of adventurers. Their immediate forbears were those whom the love of adventure drew to new and little known countries, who were not content to rust out in quiet English villages, to economize for a lifetime on oatmeal and potatoes in a Scottish croft, or to die of rheumatism on the edge of an Irish bog. They married brave girls, and crossed the long oceans to become pioneers of the newer races, transmitting their health and love of adventure to a whole nation.

The Australasians have been accustomed to the

weapons of the soldier all their lives; they are part of the daily life of many of them. The rifle and the entrenching tool pass into accustomed hands, which know just how to make the best use of them. Their far-sighted eyes detect little signs of the country through which they pass; their trained minds, versed in all the lore of the country-side, draw the just conclusions. All the work of the camp comes naturally and easily to their hands; many of them are practised guides and scouts. They find the shortest and best way from one place to another by an uncanny kind of instinct; they select the best paths by some natural process that cannot be explained.

When the Australasians were first submitted to the practical test of campaigning to prove their worth in actual warfare, they were held by experts to have failed in one particular, due to their lack of special training. One requisite of the modern soldier was wanting in their composition: they were deficient in discipline. They insisted on ignoring many of the formalities in behaviour exacted from the trained soldier; they protested that they could not see the necessity for them. It would have been easier to underestimate this disadvantage than to correct it, had the Australasians adhered to their original schemes of national defence. But before a second time of testing had come round, they had made differences

The Last March through Sydney Streets.

of a vital kind in their military system, and in the change the defect in training had been remedied.

With the introduction of national service in Australasia, provision was also made for the local production of the implements and munitions of warfare, and for military equipment. Their local supply of the raw material for such purposes is unequalled in the world, and thus it came that the Australian forces in the Great War were equipped in a style of serviceable comfort that was the admiration of all who examined it. In short, the Australasian forces who were sent to participate in the Great War were first-class material, well-trained and excellently found, a body of men of whom it was reasonable to expect fine deeds should the chance ever come their way.

The other factors to be taken into consideration are important ones. The first was their fine youthful pride in the opportunity of serving side by side with the soldiers of the Mother Country, and of the proud European nations allied to her. There will always be generous rivalry between the troops of two great nations fighting side by side in a just cause. But the spirit in which the Australasians went out to the service of the Mother Empire goes deeper and further still. It holds nothing questioning or calculated, it is the conduct of men who hail as a proud privilege the opportunity of laying down their lives for the underlying principles on which the structure of the British Empire is reared. The danger note had only to be sounded and these men hastened to record their eagerness to serve; more, they well knew why they were so keen. With them duty and inclination walked hand in hand.

Finally, the people of Australasia are well assured of the justice of the cause for which they fight. Nowhere was more interest displayed in the speeches that explained the causes to which the war is due, nowhere is there a public better informed of the efforts made to preserve peace, and of the deliberate flouting of them by Germany. Small nations themselves, the Southern Britons fully comprehend the danger to the small nations of Europe from the grasping aggression of their strong unscrupulous neighbours. They claim as part of their heritage those pages of British history which tell how gloriously Great Britain has espoused the cause of the weak in the past. There is no quarrel in which the men of Australasia would more gladly take up arms with the Mother Country than one for the innocent weak against the guilty strong. And such a quarrel, they are well persuaded, is the root cause of the Great War in which they are now fighting.

LONESOME PINE AND RUSSELL'S TOP

CHAPTER XX

LONESOME PINE AND RUSSELL'S TOP

DURING the last weeks of July the camp at Anzac was stirred by continuous talk of a resumption of offensive operations against the Turks. The Australasians were tired of the inaction that had been forced upon them. To remain tied to a small area of land on the edge of a cliff, to live under shell fire night and day, to have to submit to the loss of twenty or thirty men every day; this had been their lot for many weeks. The delay seemed to their restless spirits interminable, and the joy with which they discussed the prospect of a fresh advance can hardly be realized by those who had not shared the tedium of their dangerous inaction.

In the early days of August the rumours of a fresh advance grew to a certainty. Quietly and by night regiments of Kitchener's Army were landed at Ari Burnu, just north of Anzac Cove. They took the place of the Australasians in many of the trenches. Large stores of ammunition were concentrated at various points on the Australasian lines, and especially at one of the outposts on the extreme left, which was connected by a deep sap with the main line at Walker's Ridge. This outpost, known as Maori outpost or Outpost No. 2, was shortly to be the base for a very important series of operations.

New machine-guns, of a make unfamiliar to the Australasians, were posted in the trenches, and huge supplies of ammunition were stored at depots throughout the Anzac area. Whether the Turks were aware of these preparations cannot be known with any certainty; but it appears probable that they suspected some new move, though they were not awake to its full importance.

The strategy of the Australasians was employed in fostering the idea among their enemies that a new attack was to be developed on the right of the Australasian line. With that object in view a continuous fire was kept up on the right, and the new machine-guns, which had a totally different report to that of the maxims with which the Australasians were originally armed, were used in this locality. Finally an attack was made on a position on the right known as Tasmania Ridge, which was captured by the Australasians after a spirited Turkish resistance.

Eventually, on August 6, a series of blows was struck at the Turkish force opposite the position at

Anzac. At Suvla Bay, some five miles north of Anzac Cove, a force of some 40,000 British troops was landed under cover of darkness and of the operations carried on simultaneously by the Australasians against the Turkish force.

The net result of the operations was disclosed in an official communiqué dated August 25, and couched in the following terms :—

"The attack from Anzac, after a series of desperately contested actions, was carried to the summit of Sari Bahr and Chunuk Bahr ridges, which are the dominating positions in this area. But owing to the fact that the attack from Suvla did not make the progress which was counted on, the troops from Anzac were not able to maintain their position on the actual crest line, and, after repeated counter-attacks, were forced to withdraw to positions close below it. These positions have been consolidated effectively.

"The attack from Suvla was not developed quickly enough, and was brought to a standstill after an advance of about $2\frac{1}{2}$ miles. The ground gained by both attacks was, however, sufficient to enable their lines to be connected along a front of more than twelve miles."

The circumstances which caused the attack of the Australasians to fail from lack of support do not come within the scope of this book. It is sufficient that the official record makes it clear that the men of Anzac did all that was required of them. The generous recorders of the fighting have further placed it on record that the Australasians displayed a heroism and devotion almost without parallel in the history of modern warfare.

It will be convenient to describe first of all the fight in which the First Brigade of Australian infantry took part, which resulted in the capture of a position known as the Lonesome Pine plateau. This position was opposite the centre of the old Anzac line, rather south of Courtney's Post. There the Turks had constructed a series of defence works of great strength, and, in order to protect the foremost trenches against the bombardments to which they were liable from our warships, had roofed them in with heavy wooden sleepers, covered with a liberal quantity of earth. They were practically shell-proof trenches.

The third and fourth lines of trenches were not so protected, and upon these a heavy shell fire was directed, at daybreak on August 6, from the warships and the land batteries as well. For two hours this shelling lasted, and, as it was afterwards discovered, the rear trenches of the Turks were choked with dead and wounded; for large forces had been concentrated here for the defence of the position.

The charge was sounded when it had become fully light, and the First and Second Battalions of the First Brigade rushed forward with fixed bayonets.

A Battery of Australian Field Artillery going into Action.

Some of them stopped and tore up the sleepers which roofed in the foremost trenches, others charged on over the roofs to the communication trenches which afforded an exit to the Turks. These took the Turks in the rear; while the others, making holes for themselves through the roofing, dropped down into the darkness where the Turks were waiting for them.

The enemy, taken in front and rear, put up such a fight as the Australasian forces had never before experienced on the peninsula of Gallipoli. In the dark and fetid trenches men fought hand to hand, with bayonets and clubbed rifles, with bombs or knives or anything that came to hand. The Turks had the advantage of knowing every turn and twist of the rabbit warren which they had constructed, and fought as desperate men in the 150 yards of darkness over which these underground trenches extended.

From both sides more men came to mingle in the fight, and the passages became choked with dead and dying men. They fought there in the darkness with the corpses piled three deep under their feet. It had been said that the Turks would not resist the bayonet, but here in the darkness many Australians died of bayonet wounds, and were clubbed to death by the desperate men they had taken in front and rear. Finally, the Turks were driven out of the underground trenches and an attack was delivered upon the positions behind them.

Here again the Turks stood up to their enemies, and fought with the bayonet. They had little option, for those who tried to flee through the open were caught by fire from well-posted machine-guns, and mown down in scores. Some hundreds of them were driven into incompleted saps of their own digging, and forced to surrender. For three days and nights the fighting for the position continued.

The trenches were so cumbered with the dead that they were piled up shoulder high, and held in place by ropes, so that a passage might be kept clear on the other side of the trench. All the horrors of modern explosives helped to make that fight more hideous ; the rending of deadly bombs in confined places, the rattle of machine-guns that cut off from desperate men the last hopes of retreat. Men who lived through that fight will preserve to their dying day a new estimate of the horror of war under such conditions. It was possibly the fiercest hand-to-hand fight even in the history of the Great War.

It ended in the capture of the Turkish position and the burial of between 1,000 and 1,200 Turkish dead. The victors were relieved by the Second Brigade of Australian infantry, who consolidated the position. It is still held by the Australasian forces, in spite of a shell fire directed upon it night and day from all conceivable points of the compass. Not only had an important position been won, but the Australasians had again emphasized their fighting superiority over the Turks.

At the same time there was being enacted, farther to the left, one of the greatest tragedies which had befallen the Australasians during their occupation of the Anzac Zone. The participants were two battalions of the Australian Light Horse; the 8th (Victoria), and the 10th (West Australia). Both were practically wiped out in a gallant attack upon a very strong Turkish position, opposite the highest point of Walker's Ridge, known as Russell's Top. At this point the Turkish trenches approached nearer to those of the Australasians than at any other point on the left of the Australasian position. The Australasian trenches were opposed by a high slope, known to the men as " Baby 600," and up this the Turks had constructed a series of trenches, each of which was commanded by the wings of that behind, after the approved Turkish fashion. It was afterwards found that a large number of machine-guns were skilfully posted in defence of the position. The number is estimated by some of the men who were there at forty.

Against this position, after a heavy bombardment of it by our warships had taken place, the 8th Light Horse were sent early on the morning of August 7. The distance they had to cross to reach the first Turkish trench was only twenty-five yards in the centre of the position, and extended to sixty yards on the wings. When they emerged from their trenches to attack, they were met with such a tornado of bullets from rifles and machine-guns that only one man of them reached the Turkish trench, which he never left. The rest of the story is revealed by the casualty sheets of the 8th Light Horse.

During the morning that followed the Turkish trench was so bombarded with high explosive shells that it became no longer tenable, being almost entirely filled in. The bombardment ceased suddenly, and the 10th Light Horse was sent out to take the trench. They crossed the intervening space like a flash, and dropped down in the hollow that had once been a Turkish trench. There they lay for two hours, unable to do anything to better their position; for to lift a head or an arm was to court disaster.

The position was clearly an untenable one, and finally the men were told to retire. They made their way back across the space that separated them from their former trench under concentrated fire of the most deadly description. Half of them were fated never to reach the trench; while those who did so found it bristling with the bayonets of their own supports. As they ran they cried out, and waved down the parapet of steel, but many of them were checked within a foot of safety by the weapons of their own friends, and killed by Turkish bullets.

Such are the grim outlines of the disaster which

A Typical Trooper of the Australian Light Horse.

overtook the Light Horse. The difficulties and the strength of the position they attacked had long been known, not only to them, but to every Australasian posted on the left of the Anzac lines. It says much for their devotion that there was no sign of hanging back when they were ordered to attack a series of trenches notorious for their stiff defences among the war-wise men of Anzac Cove.

THE MIGHTY NEW ZEALANDERS

CHAPTER XXI

THE MIGHTY NEW ZEALANDERS

IN preceding chapters little mention has been made of the men of New Zealand since we saw them charging up the hill at Krithia in full view of the soldiers of half the world. Their share of the fighting at Anzac was nevertheless an important one; they had to defend the extreme left of the Australasian lines. This comprised the line of hills known as Walker's Ridge, facing almost due north, and especially the summit of this ridge, where the Australian lines made a sharp angle near Pope's Hill. During the month of July, too, the New Zealanders took over the defence of Quinn's Post, and by dint of very skilful sapping operations made that once dangerous post one of the safest places in the whole camp.

Farther north than Walker's Ridge itself, the New Zealanders also held two isolated posts known as Outpost No. 1 and Outpost No. 2. Communication with the main lines from these outposts was maintained through deep saps, which had been dug by the New Zealanders themselves. Of these Outposts No. 2 was held by the 500 Maori soldiers attached to the New Zealand Contingent, and was sometimes known as Maori Outpost. This place was used as a base for stores; and here in the first days of August an immense amount of munitions and food was accumulated.

And at this outpost, during the night of August 5, the men of New Zealand and the Fourth Brigade of Australian infantry were massed for the attack which was delivered on August 6. Still farther north was another post called Outpost No. 3, which had long been disputed by the opposing forces. Between this point and the lower slopes of the great hill of Sari Bair (marked on the maps as Hill 971) were a number of high points, chief among which were Bauchop's Hill and two flat-topped hills known as Greater and Lesser Tabletop. The sides of these Tabletop hills were almost perpendicular, and the Turks had adorned their summits with such a network of trenches as to make them impregnable, if held by any considerable force of men. But in the early days of August it was known that very few men occupied these defensive trenches, and one of the objects of the attack of August 6 was to take these positions by surprise.

After night had fallen on August 6, the New Zealanders and the 4th Brigade of Australians marched out from Maori Outpost, stepping silently

A Battalion of New Zealand Mounted Rifles

through the scrub in a northerly direction. From the beach a series of gullies, running at right angles to the shore, give an entry to the hill slopes that lead up to the main ridges of Sari Bair and Chunuk Bair, which are the highest points of the mountain mass, and are separated by a deep ravine.

Up these gullies the New Zealanders made their way, clearing the enemy out of the trenches he had dug to bar the approaches to Sari Bair. Charging up one gully, the men of Wellington surprised and captured the Tabletop hills. Up a parallel gully the Auckland Mounted Rifles went, to take possession of Rhododendron Ridge. The Maoris charged up yet a third gully, to take Bauchop's Hill and the trenches beyond it. The impetuosity of their charge carried them through a depression communicating between their own gully and that up which the men of Auckland had passed.

They came over a spur of the hills, yelling with excitement, and seeing in the dim light that a trench before them was occupied by armed men, rushed upon it, shouting their war cry. The men before them were the men of Auckland, who at once recognized the war cries of the Maoris. Fortunately the average New Zealander rather prides himself upon possessing a fair smattering of the Maori tongue, and this knowledge came in very handy as the Maoris charged down upon their own friends.

The Auckland men shouted at them what phrases of Maori they could summon up in such an emergency, and the Maori charge was stayed on the very parapet of the trench itself.

The beginning of that fierce charge of Maoris, when they swept every Turk out of their path, was described to me by a New Zealander who was present, in the following words:—

"We lay under cover in the dark waiting for the word to go. Every man had his bayonet fixed and his magazine empty. The work before us had to be done with the cold steel. The Turks had three lines of trenches on the hill slope opposite.

"Suddenly I became aware of a stir among the Maoris on my left; I was right up against them. Next to me was a full-blooded Maori chief, a young fellow of sixteen stone, as big and powerful as a bullock. I played Rugby against him once and tried to tackle him; it was as much use as trying to stop a rushing elephant. He is a lineal descendant of fighting Rewi, the Maori chief from whom all the legends descend.

"You know the story of Rewi. Once he and his tribe were surrounded in a Pah by a force of white men who outnumbered them three to one. The whites had got between them and the stream of water on the top of the hill, which is unfair fighting according to Maori rules. Then they sent a message to Rewi bidding him surrender. He replied, 'Ka

Whawhai Tonu, Aké Aké Aké.' ('We fight on and on; for ever and for ever and for ever.') 'Then send away the women and children,' was the next suggestion. 'The women fight too,' says brave old Rewi. An hour later the Maoris rushed out of the Pah with Rewi at the head of them and before the astonished whites knew what was doing had cut a way through and escaped.

"This descendant of Rewi's is a different sort of chap. He holds two good university degrees and is one of the finest speakers in New Zealand. Not much more than a year ago I saw him in a frock coat and a silk hat, with creases in his pants that would have cut cheese, telling a lot of bush Maoris of the virtues of cleanliness and the nobility of hard work.

"But now he had dressed for the occasion in a pair of running shoes and shorts which covered about eight inches of the middle of him. I could see the whites of his eyes gleaming and his brown skin glistening with perspiration in the dim light. His head was moving from side to side and his lips were twitching. From time to time he beat the earth softly with his clenched fist.

"Then I got the swing of it. I suppose the 500 Maoris picked me up into their silent war song." For I know the words of the Haka well, and though they could not dance it they were beating out the measure of it with their fists on the ground. There they lay, and after each soft thump I could feel that their bodies strained forward like dogs on a leash. They caught me up in their madness and I longed to be at it. I thumped the ground with them, and prayed to be up and dancing, or out and fighting.

"Would the whistle never blow?

"Now their eyes were rolling and their breath was coming in long, rhythmical sobs. The groaning sound of it was quite audible; in another minute they would have been up on their feet, dancing their wild war dance. But then came the signal; and Hell was let loose.

"'Aké, Aké,' they shouted, 'we fight for ever and for ever.' Up to the first trench they swept, and we gave them the right of way. It was their privilege. I could hear some of them yelling, 'Kiki ta Turk' ('Kick the Turk'). Those were the fellows who had kept on their heaviest boots, and meant to use their feet. God help the Turk who got a kick from a war-mad Maori.

"Our own blood was up; I know mine was. We were not far behind them to the first trench, and you never saw such a sight in your life. The Turks had been bashed to death; there is no other word for it. We got up to them at the second trench, where there was a deadly hand-to-hand going on. Some of them had broken their rifles and were fighting with their hands. I saw one

Maori smash a Turk with half-a-hundred-weight of rock he had torn up. I don't remember much more, because now I was in it myself. That is why I am here.

"I don't know anything more at first hand. I hear a good many of them came back, though I shouldn't have thought it possible. I am also told they were very pleased with themselves, as they have had good reason to be. The Turks who escaped from them will not wait another time when they hear the Maoris coming; that I'll answer for. And you can hear them coming all right."

By such wild fighting the men of New Zealand steadily won their way upwards, through all the tangle of gullies and steep hillsides that leads to the crest of the big hill. By day they hung on doggedly to the positions they had won, resisting attacks delivered with bayonet and bomb. By night they moved stealthily on, through dense scrub and badly broken country, converging by parallel paths toward the desired crest of the hill.

No words can paint the gallantry of the fighting of the four days that followed the night of August 6. August 9 saw a gallant little band of New Zealanders planting their artillery flags on the trench that spans the summit of Chunuk Bair, while a little later the Gurkhas, who had occupied a gully still farther north than those penetrated by the New Zealanders, arrived on the crest of 971 itself.

From that point of vantage the bold pioneers could see all they had striven for through many weary weeks of constant fighting. Away to the south-east were the forts of the Narrows. At their very feet ran the road of communication, which leads from Gallipoli town to the main Turkish position at Achi Baba. They could see the trains of mules and the transport vehicles passing along this road. The goal of their efforts was there, in their full sight.

Right and left, on higher crests, were the Turks in force, determined to drive them from their post of vantage. Desperately the New Zealanders hung on to what they had gained, until support should come. The history of that attempt to hold a hilltop is one of the most glorious in all the annals of war. Some day the world will know how sixteen New Zealanders kept a long section of trench against a whole host of enemies for three hours. It may even be told how and why the position was abandoned. If the desperate valour of the men of New Zealand, and of their Gurkha friends, could have conserved it, it would never have been lost. Eventually, for no fault of theirs, the New Zealanders had to retire. They would rather have died where they were ; a good many of them did so.

The losses of those four days can best be judged by reference to the casualty lists. The Auckland

Mounted Rifles, who went out 800 strong on the day of August 6, had a roll-call on August 11. One who was present told me that twenty-two men only answered to their names. Afterwards the number of uninjured was raised to thirty-seven by men who came back from the help of the wounded.

The New Zealand wounded had an experience that is an epic of suffering. Only the supreme fortitude with which it was endured impels me to give some account of the days and nights spent by over four hundred of these heroes in a place which they have christened the Valley of Torment. It was placed on the rugged side of Sari Bair, a deep depression in the hillside. On one side of it a mountain wall rose in a perpendicular cliff that would have defied a mountain goat to climb it. On the other rose the steep declivity of Rhododendron Ridge. Below, the valley opened out upon a flat plateau, so swept by the guns of both sides that no living thing could exist for one moment upon its flat, clear surface.

The only way in and out of the valley was from above, where the New Zealanders were fighting like possessed beings for the foothold they had won on the crest of Sari Bair. And to this valley the stretcher-bearers had carried the men who had fallen in the fight, a sad little group of wounded men whose numbers were hourly increasing. There, too, crawled those who were less severely injured.

And there the unwounded soldiers carried their stricken mates for shelter from the hail of bullets, while the fight lasted.

As the wounded men came in, a devoted band of Red Cross men lent them what aid they could. There was no doctor nearer than the dressing station on the beach, but these Red Cross workers stayed their wounds with bandages, tying tourniquets round limbs to check the flow of arterial blood, and making tortured men as easy as circumstances would permit.

The approach to this valley was so dangerous that no one might come to it by daylight. There was no water there, until one man, less severely wounded than some of his comrades, dug into a moist spot far down the valley, and chanced on a spring that yielded a thin trickle of brackish water.

By midday on August 8 there were three hundred wounded men in this place of refuge, and more were continually arriving. They were suffering from all the terrible manglings that exploding bombs and high explosive shells can inflict. And in the Valley of Torment they lay and endured. Some of them told their experiences, and sought to cheer the rest by predicting a great victory as the result of the attack in which they were taking part. Here and there a man could be heard reciting verses to those who would listen.

No one moaned, and no one uttered a complaint.

When a man too sorely wounded died of his hurts, they expressed their thanks that he had been spared further pain. The filling of the little spring was eagerly awaited, so that each man could have his lips moistened with a little brackish water. So there they lay and waited for the night, which might bring them aid.

When night at last came, the weary stretcher-bearers tried to move some of them over the ridge to a safe valley which lay on the other side. A few were so moved, but these men had been working for days and nights without rest or respite, and the task was beyond their strength; for the steepness and roughness of that hillside is beyond description. A message was sent down to the dressing station asking for help, and a reply was sent in the early morning that it would be forthcoming on the following night.

Through the night the parched men were tortured by the sight of water being carried through the valley to the men in the firing line above them. There was none of it for them, and they did not expect any; for they knew the necessities of warfare, and recognized that at such a time the combatant must come first.

The next day came with a hot sun, and clouds of flies. Also there came many more wounded to the Valley of Torment, until the tale of living men exceeded four hundred. And that day many died.

Among those who lived the torture from tourniquets that had been left too long on wounded limbs became unendurable. Many of them will never recover the free use of the limbs so tortured; others have already died from the unavoidable mortification which resulted from this long delay.

Meanwhile, down at the dressing stations, the weary doctors were struggling with hundreds of cases just as bad, and men seriously wounded were waiting by scores for their turn for attention. These are the necessary evils of war, accentuated at Gallipoli by the very rough nature of the country in which the fighting took place, and by the severity of the struggle and the importance of the issues depending upon its outcome.

At last that day ended too, and evening fell with a cool breeze. The exhausted men heard the stealthy approach of many men in the dark, from the safe gully that lay beyond the range. And one of them, out of thankfulness, began to sing the hymn—

> At even, ere the sun was set,
> The sick, O Lord, around Thee lay.

Nearly all of them took up the singing.

While they were still singing, there came over the ridge a large number of soldiers, and put them all on stretchers. Then the new-comers, some thousands in number, ranged themselves in two rows facing one another. The double row of soldiers stretched up to the crest of the ridge, and down the other side into the safe gully that was there. And each stretcher was passed from hand to hand, up the steep ridge and down the slope to the safety that lay on the other side.

When all had been taken from the Valley of Torment, a long procession of men with stretchers was formed, bearing the wounded down to the sea. Two miles it stretched from start to finish, and it serpentined slowly down the gully, each pair of bearers walking with slow care, for the sake of the tortured man who was in their charge.

So the wounded men of New Zealand were carried out of the Valley of Torment. One could fill whole volumes about the tender care of the lightly wounded for their more grievously injured comrades, and of the stoical indifference to pain and personal suffering shown by these men. I have met many of the men who suffered there ; and I know that in their eyes the real tragedy of the experience is not the torture they experienced. It is that, after all, their comrades eventually had to forgo the advantage that had been won by so much hardihood and loss of life.

THE NIGHT MARCH,—AND
AFTERWARDS

CHAPTER XXII

THE NIGHT MARCH,—AND AFTERWARDS

THE operations against Lonesome Pine and Russell's Top, and the storming of the crest of Sari Bair, had been accompanied by a landing of British troops at Suvla Bay which had been but feebly opposed by the Turks. The task of establishing touch with this newly landed force was entrusted to the Fourth Brigade of Australian infantry, and the Wellington (New Zealand) infantry. These forces, like the New Zealanders who stormed Sari Bair, had their base at Outpost No. 2 ; and from that point marched north in five parallel columns during the night of August 6.

Their line of march lay north-east, through unknown country that was badly broken by gullies and steep hills. Their objective was the open plain which lay between Sari Bair and Suvla Bay, an agricultural plain comparatively flat and clear, where the Australasians had watched the Turkish peasants getting in their crops through the month of July.

It was the individual resource and confidence of

each unit of these Colonial troops which permitted this difficult night march to be accomplished successfully. The task of co-operation set to the newly landed troops at Suvla Bay was by no means so difficult. Without intending any disparagement of these forces, it has to be said that if they had displayed the initiative and resource of their more seasoned Colonial comrades, a more successful outcome of these operations could surely have been recorded.

The plan adopted by the Australians was beautiful in its simplicity, and in the full reliance placed upon each individual man. The officers showed the non-commissioned men their maps of the unknown country through which the night march was to be made; and the non-coms. in their turn explained to each man the object of the march, and the nature of the chief obstacles marked on the maps.

When the word to advance was given, the men simply melted away into the darkness, and without any noise made their way towards the goal. Sometimes two or three pressed forward silently together; more often the fellows made their way alone. The most impressive part of that advance was its noiselessness. Now and then the enemy would turn their guns down the gullies up which the advance was being made, and then each man found cover as best he could, and waited until he thought it safe to pursue his onward way.

The net result of these tactics was that a surprisingly large percentage of the men reached their objective unharmed. Where opposition had to be overcome, the men massed silently in the darkness, and charged at the word of their officers. The terror inspired among the Turks by these midnight charges, coming suddenly out of the silent darkness, has been testified by the prisoners taken.

Thus the Fourth Brigade reached its objective after the wonderful night march; but the expected supports were not forthcoming. During the day that followed, the enemy appeared in great force, and there was some stiff fighting. The 13th Brigade captured the emplacement of a 75-gun, which had worked great havoc during the preceding six weeks in the Australasian trenches. The 15th Battalion saw the gun disappearing round one long bend of a valley, as they emerged from the scrub at the elbow below. A few shots were fired at it, but the chance was lost, by at most two minutes.

The 14th Brigade captured a Turkish bakery, and a Turkish major in charge of it; also a telephone exchange and a very sullen German lieutenant. Later in the day the 16th Battalion encountered a strong force of the enemy, very skilfully posted, and suffered very severe losses.

The advance was continued through the night in the direction of the village called Biyuk Anafarta, the white mosque of which had always been a landmark to the Australasians, where it gleamed among the gloomy cypress trees that surround it. On August 8 the Fourth Brigade effected a juncture with the force from Suvla Bay, and the British line extended along the coast from Gaba Tepe to Suvla Bay, a distance of twelve miles.

But the object of the operations of the Brigade, which was to surprise the strong positions between Sari Bair and Anafarta village, had been defeated by the delay. The Turks were posted strongly on two positions here known as Hill 60 and Hill 70, and the necessary support to the bold assailers of Sari Bair could not be rendered. The Fourth Brigade, like their comrades elsewhere, had lost heavily in the three days' fighting which followed the night march.

A few days later they were supported by the Fifth Brigade of Australian infantry, which landed from Egypt on August 19. So strengthened, they delivered a fresh attack on Hill 60 on August 21. Here again the fighting was fierce and determined; but the Australians would not be denied. Eventually they captured the hill, only to be driven from it by the violent counter-attacks of the Turks delivered in great numbers.

On August 27, a fresh attack was made on Hill 60, in which the Fifth Brigade played a conspicuous part. On the same occasion the Suvla Bay forces made a fine attack on Hill 70, which they stormed

Australian Guns in Action before Sari Bair.

and held. And there the record of the operations in this part of the peninsula of Gallipoli becomes blurred. The soldiers who returned wounded after the fighting at the end of August gave the most optimistic accounts of the position. They are discounted to a large extent by the statement made by Lord Kitchener in the House of Lords on September 15.

In describing the operations at Suvla Bay the Minister for War said:—

"The attack from Anzac, after a series of hotly contested actions, was carried to the summit of Sari Bair and Chunuk Bair, which are the dominating positions in this area. The arrival of the transports and the disembarkation of the troops in Suvla Bay were designed to enable the troops to support this attack. Unfortunately, however, the advance from Suvla was not developed quickly enough and the movement forward was brought to a standstill after an advance of about $2\frac{1}{2}$ miles. The result was that the troops from Anzac were unable to retain their position on the crest of the hills, and after being repeatedly counter-attacked they were ordered to withdraw to positions lower down.

"These positions, however, have been effectively consolidated, and now, joining with the line occupied by the Suvla Bay force, form a connected front of more than twelve miles. From the latter position a further attack on the Turkish entrenchment was delivered on August 21, but after several hours of sharp fighting *it was not found possible to gain the summit of the hills occupied by the enemy, and the intervening space being unsuitable for defence the troops were withdrawn to their original position.*

" Since then comparative quiet has prevailed and a much-needed rest has been given to our troops. In the course of these operations the gallantry and resourcefulness of the Australian and New Zealand troops have frequently formed a subject for eulogy in Sir Ian Hamilton's reports. General Birdwood and his staff have greatly distinguished themselves both in planning and conducting the operations of the Australian and New Zealand Corps, whose activities have been marked by constant success. Their determination to overcome apparently insuperable difficulties has been no less admirable than their courage in hand-to-hand fighting with the enemy.

" It is not easy to appreciate at their full value the enormous difficulties which have attended the operations in the Dardanelles or the fine temper with which our troops have met them. *There is now abundant evidence of a process of demoralization having set in among the German-led (or rather German-driven) Turks*, due, no doubt, to their extremely heavy losses and to the progressive failure of their resources. It is only fair to acknowledge that, judged from a humane point of view, the methods of warfare pursued by the Turks are vastly superior to those which disgraced their German masters."

The end of August saw the area of the Anzac zone increased to three times the extent of the original holding. It also witnessed a concentration of Turkish shell fire upon the whole area. The testimony of the men who have returned to Great Britain to be cured of their wounds, shows that the Turkish ammunition now in use is of very inferior quality. Of six 10-inch shells which fell around one dressing station on an August day, only one exploded. All had apparently come from the big guns in the forts at the Narrows.

The constant use of old-fashioned muzzle-loading guns of heavy calibre is also a sign of waning stores of munitions. These guns throw a round 100-pound ball which the Australasians call "plum-puddings" or "footballs." They advertise their arrival by a sound which resembles "the loud song of a bird," and are clearly visible as they come hurtling through the air.

For this reason they are not much feared, the whole of Australasian apprehension being reserved for the shells of the 75's; which come noiselessly, and announce their arrival only by the sharp crack of their explosion.

No Australasian will dispute the dictum that at the end of August the firing-line was the safest place in the Anzac zone. The vast majority of casualties occurred to men who were supposed to be spelling. But the Australasians were so conscious of the Turkish demoralization described by Lord Kitchener that they were looking forward eagerly to yet another resumption of the offensive in the zone which they established on the shores of Gallipoli Peninsula.

THE BAND OF BROTHERS

CHAPTER XXIII

THE BAND OF BROTHERS

AN Australian officer had been telling me of the remarkable bravery of two men of his company, and I asked the natural question : " Did you report them for recognition ? " " No," was the answer. " They did no more than their duty ; no more than any other two of my men would have done in similar circumstances." That answer will serve to explain why, among a force which has lost nearly half its men by death or wounds, and which has carried on war with a reckless bravery that has excited the admiration of the whole world, only one Victoria Cross has been won ; and why the other awards for services of an exceptional nature have been singularly few.

But the feeling that underlay that reply cuts far deeper than the award of crosses and orders. It proclaims the Australasians for what they are, a band of devoted brothers, fighting for something far dearer to them than public recognition. I will allow the same officer to tell what kind of men they were, and to describe the mutual love and respect that animated them as a band in the worst of their days in Gallipoli. He said :—

"The Australian soldier is often said to be lacking in discipline. Well, it all depends what you call discipline. Let me give you an example. When we landed the men were ordered to advance with fixed bayonets and do the work with the cold steel. They were not to fire unless it was absolutely necessary. Days afterwards we found some of our men out in the bad country around Quinn's Post dead with their rifles beside them; the bayonets fixed and not a round fired. They had obeyed orders until the last, because they were good orders. They must have had innumerable temptations to loose off their rifles, but they died like soldiers, with red-tipped bayonets and clean barrels. I call that discipline.

"On August 7 our fellows were relieved in the firing line by a draft of Kitchener's men. The scrub around was stiff with snipers, all eager to pick off an officer or two for choice. Yet here were these chaps saluting every officer who looked at them; saluting like clockwork. Our major is a peppery chap who rose from the ranks in the African war. 'What the blue fire do you mean by it ?' he roared at one of the 'Kitchener's.' 'Do you want to have me killed ?' They simply couldn't understand him. Now you may call that discipline, but I do not. I call it rank foolishness, and worse.

"The reputation of the major was that he never threw away a life and never risked his own unnecessarily. Yet he was always risking his own, and the men would follow him anywhere. He had only to speak to get the most implicit obedience. One day he said, 'Look here, men! Some English staff officers are coming to see you this afternoon. Shave yourselves and try to look smart if you can. And, for Heaven's sake, don't call me Alf.' My word, they did him proud that day.

"I see some of them now, with their hard faces shaded by their slouched hats, and I remember them a grousing, cursing crowd in the transport, and I think to myself, 'Can these be the uncomplaining, unselfish, God-fearing heroes I fought with at Courtney's Post?' I tell you that battle turned those fellows' best side outermost. Having seen their best side I can never pay any attention to the other side of them as long as I live. They made me proud to belong to the same race as they, and more than proud to be entrusted with the command of such splendid men.

"Their bravery had as many facets as a well-cut diamond. But the side I admired most was their sheer grit. The first five days in the firing line they had no sleep at all, and were fighting every minute of the time. They had no food except some dirty water and a few hard biscuits. On the evening of the fifth day the C.O. came into the trench and said, 'Boys, you've stuck it splendidly, and now you're going to be relieved. I've got you some hot tea that will come round in a minute or two, and shortly after you will be relieved. And they answered, 'Only get us some tea, sir, and we'll stick it as long as you like.'

"Their hard, stern-lipped faces will never more blind me to the big, soft hearts they mask so effec-tually. One day I was resting in a bit of a dug-out, sopping wet, shaking with a feerish cold, no great-coat or blanket or cover of any kind. I was not feeling very good. A great big fellow went toiling up the hill, pulling himself from one tree to the other by the branches, the only way to get up. He had got some way past me when he caught sight of me. I suppose I looked very wretched. Back he came with the good word, 'Feeling knocked out, matey?' asks he. 'Never mind, you buck up and -- Oh, I beg pardon, sir'. A day or two later he came up to me and again began to apologize. To apologize, when he had done me more good than i had imagined anything short of aquick and painless death could have done!

"We had a young subaltern from Duntroon College, as gallant a boy as ever looked death in the face, and that he did every hour of the day and night for weeks. He commanded men old enough to be his father, and he was the darling of their hearts. One day the inevitable happened and he went down (to the sea front) with a big hole in him. Some days afterwards his men were going back to rest camp and they came to me to inquire after him. I can see them now, half a score of as unsavoury-looking ruffians as ever could be seen. Their faces were shaggy with two weeks' beard and their eyes were red and bulging with unintermittent vigils. They had cheated death for yet another week. And the tears ran down their cheeks as they begged to know if ' there was any chance for the Boy.' Men like that stir your innermost fibre.

"I have seen those men shepherding that boy in the trenches in all sorts of ways. I have seen them standing between him and the place from where the rifle fire was coming and he did not know it. One man, to my certain knowledge, was hit that way. I charged him with it in the dug-out—he was not badly wounded—and he gave me the lie in the most emphatic Australian fashion. I don't know what discipline demanded of me, but I do know that I shook hands and whispered to him that I would never tell the boy. And he grinned and winked like the jolly old bushman he was.

"Some of them were pretty rough, but it is wonderful how they yield to the refining fire of battle. There was one trench where the language was pretty sulphurous. One day they lost their lieutenant, a great favourite, by a shell which wounded him mortally and kicked a lot of sandbags on top of him. The men set to work like maniacs, pulling away the sandbags and cursing horribly. He heard them and said, 'Don't swear, men; that does no good.' They were his last words. It is a fact that an oath in that trench was a worse crime than cowardice from that day forward.

"The best laugh we had for six weeks came out of the lurid language used by Tommy Cornstalk. Our post was at the head of a deep gully between two high hills and there were places in that gully where the weirdest echoes lived. A few words spoken at one of these spots would ring through the hills for a minute after and eventually die away in a ghostly whisper. After the great armistice near the end of May we had good reason to know that the enemy had been using their eyes to some purpose. They had new lines of fire, and places that were safe before the armistice were deadly dangerous afterwards. I suppose that is part of the game of war.

"While the armistice was on two platoons were down in the rest camp, and when they came back none had told the men of the altered state of affairs. Next morning two of these fellows were basking in the sun on the hillside, drinking hot tea and smoking. As far as they knew the place was quite safe. I was just going to call out to them, when the first bullet arrived. It kicked up a great patch of dust between them. Both men jumped down simultaneously, a drop of 20 feet, and as they jumped both made the same emphatic remark. The echoes took it up and passed it along in a sort of monotonous repetition. We stood spellbound to hear the immortal hills of Gallipoli repeating to one another the round oaths of the Australian backblocks in a shocked whisper.

" When it was all over it was like the curtain going down on an excruciatingly funny scene in a theatre. The men were all strung very high by the events through which they had lived, and they gave themselves up to laughter that was almost hysterical. In the middle of it the Turks in the trench opposite began to blaze away as if cartridges cost nothing, and that made us laugh harder than ever. We held our sides and yelled. An hour afterwards you could see men wiping the tears from their cheeks and thumping their mates on the back, and telling them not to be blooming fools. Then they would all start over again.

"We had a good many brothers in our battalion, and it was touching to see the anxiety of the elders for their younger brothers. One fellow was a signalman, and if I say that the casualty average among signalmen was 100 per cent., I am guilty of only the slightest exaggeration. His young brother was about the youngest man there, and we had him in a place where he was as safe as possible, in such circumstances. I used to hear this fellow come in at night from his signalling work, where his life wasn't worth an hour's purchase, and the first thing he would say was always: 'Is Hal all right?' I tell you he would wring my heart. I used to lie in my dug-out waiting for that question and fearing I would not hear it. For it was not Hal that I was worrying about.

"I remember the last service the battalion had before we landed. We were steaming past Cape Helles to Anzac, the untried soldiers of a new country preparing for our first battle ordeal. The warships were roaring together to cover the British landing at Cape Helles, and the padre gathered the men together for a simple service and talk. One thing he told them that sank in. The band, who were also the stretcher-bearers, had come in for a lot of chaff, as non-combatants. 'And the time is at hand,' says the padre, 'when you'll want to bite off your tongues for every idle word you've said to the band.' If ever words of man came true those words did. Ask any Australian who were the bravest men at Anzac, and you are sure to get the unhesitating answer, 'The stretcher-bearers.'

"I have seen them carrying wounded men down those hills up which we pulled ourselves by ropes passed from tree to tree. The bullets were spitting all around them, and they were checking and going slow, their only concern being not to shake the tortured man they were carrying. I know an officer whom they carried down through shell fire, and every time they heard a shell coming these two men put down the stretcher and threw themselves across his body to protect him from the shrapnel. The proportion of their dead and wounded in the casualty lists shows how these non-combatants did their work. Jokes about the band are not popular any longer; they never were very funny."

Perhaps the most famous of all the stretcher-bearers at Anzac was the ubiquitous hero known to every Australasian there as the Man with the Donkey. They were a quaint couple. The man was a 6 ft. Australian, hard-bitten and active. His gaunt profile spoke of wide experience of hard struggles in rough places. The donkey was a little mouse-coloured animal, no taller than a Newfoundland dog. His master called him Abdul. The man seemed to know by intuition every twist and slope of the tortuous valleys of Sari Bair. The donkey was a patient, sure-footed ally, with a capacity for bearing loads out of all proportion to his size.

Some days they would bring in as many as twelve or fifteen men, gathered at infinite risk in the dangerous broken country around far-out Quinn's Post. Every trip saw them face the terrors of the Valley of Death; here all day and all night the air sang with the bullets from the Turkish snipers hidden on Dead Man's Ridge. Their partnership began on the second day of occupation of the Anzac zone of Gallipoli. The man had carried two heavy men in succession down the awful slopes of Shrapnel Gully and through the Valley of Death. His eye lit on the donkey. "I'll take this chap with me next trip," he said, and from that time the pair were inseparable.

When the enfilading fire down the valley was at its worst and orders were posted that the ambulance men must not go out, the Man and the Donkey continued placidly at their work. At times they held trenches of hundreds of men spellbound, just to see them at their work. Their quarry lay motionless in an open patch, in easy range of a dozen Turkish rifles. Patiently the little donkey waited under cover, while the man crawled through the thick scrub until he got within striking distance. Then a lightning dash, and he had the wounded man on his back and was making for cover again. In those fierce seconds he always seemed to bear a charmed life.

Once in cover he tended his charge with quick, skilful movements. "He had hands like a woman's," said one who thinks he owes his life to the man and the donkey. Then the limp form was balanced across the back of the patient animal, and, with a slap on its back and the Arab donkey-boy's cry of "Gee," the man started off for the beach, the donkey trotting unruffled by his side.

For a month and more they continued their work. No one kept count of the number of wounded men they brought back from the firing line. One morning the dressers at the station near the dangerous turn in the valley called "The Pump" saw them go past, and shouted a warning to the man. The Turks up on Dead Man's Ridge were very busy that day; moreover, a machine-gun was turned on a dangerous part of the valley path. The man replied to the warning with a wave of his hand. Later he was seen returning, the donkey laden with one wounded man and the man carrying another. As they reached the dangerous turn the machine-gun rattled out, and the man fell with a bullet through his heart. The donkey walked unscathed into safety.

There was a hush through the Australian trenches that night, when the news went round that the Man with the Donkey had "got it."

His grave bears the rough inscription:—

"Sacred to the memory of Private W. Simpson, of the Third Field Ambulance, West Australia."

But if you wish an Australian to tell you his story, you must ask for the Man with the Donkey.

A TRIBUTE TO THE TURK

CHAPTER XXIV

A TRIBUTE TO THE TURK

IN his speech delivered in the House of Lords on September 15, the Minister for War said: "It is only fair to acknowledge that, judged from a humane point of view, the methods of warfare pursued by the Turks are vastly superior to those which disgraced their German masters."

The unanimous testimony of the Australasians supports this statement of Lord Kitchener. The decency and fairness with which the Turk makes war came as a pleasant surprise to the Australasians, who had been led to expect something so entirely different that they landed on Gallipoli with very stern resolves. My own cousin, a private in the 2nd Brigade, has told me that he and all his mates had determined to end their lives, rather than fall into the hands of the Turks as prisoners. A similar resolve was carried out by many an Australasian soldier in the first weeks of the fighting. Yet the testimony of the Australasians who fell into Turkish hands is now to hand and shows that they are treated with remarkable consideration.

The rumours of Turkish atrocities were rapidly dissipated, and the Australasian soldier soon got to respect the Turk as a brave man and fair fighter. The fact that a hospital ship was always moored off Anzac Cove within easy range of the Turkish guns, and was never known to suffer, is prima facie evidence to the Australasians of the honesty of Turkish intentions. The consideration shown to their wounded general, mentioned elsewhere in this book, made a deep impression in the Australasian ranks. The prevailing opinion of the Turk is now a very favourable one; and I will let one of the Australian friends I have made in British hospitals voice it on behalf of his comrades.

"Foreign travel expands the mind," sententiously observed Trooper Billy Clancy, of the Australian Light Horse. "I had to travel in a troopship to Gallipoli to learn that all I thought I knew about the Turk was not so. Many's the time I didn't know anything at all about Turks. I expected to find a lot of jelly-bellies in baggy trousers and turned-up slippers, with gaspipe guns and hooked noses. I thought they'd be cruel cowards, rotten shots, and easy marks. I thought I was going to serve it up hot to the men with the bull's-wool whiskers. And that was just where I was wrong; I know better now.

"To begin with, my friend Bismillah is quite as well equipped as anyone else for modern war.

He has a better rifle than we have, if anything. I have two scars on my left forearm that show he knows how to use it. He carries plenty of cartridges, and in his pockets two or three up-to-date bombs guaranteed to hurt the other fellow. Sometimes he paints his face green and lets on that he is a tree. Sometimes he quits his trench and pretends he is a mountain goat, trying for a record in the hill-climbing class. But he's a soldier all the time—a born soldier and a brave one. Fighting for home and country dear is meat and drink to him.

"They used to say the Turks were cruel and tortured the wounded. No Australian believes that at Anzac now. Why, there was a Turk in the trenches opposite us at Russell's Top that we used to call Fatty Burns. Of course, that was not his name, but we called him that because he looked so much like Fatty Burns that kept the Ninety-mile shanty on the road to Winton. He had the same short beard and Roman nose, the same bright black eye and a benevolent expression as much as to say, 'I wouldn't lamb a bushman down.' This Turk was the dead spit of Fatty—like brothers they were.

"He was always sticking up his head and getting fired at. Then he would signal a miss and laugh like one o'clock. You could hear him quite plain, for the trenches were only twenty-five yards apart.

At last the fellows gave up shooting at him. 'It's only Fatty Burns,' they used to say. We got to look for his cheerful grin, and sometimes we used to fire just to hear him laugh.

"One morning early, we made a bit of a demonstration, and left two of our boys wounded out on an open space between the trenches. No one could go to them, and there they lay in the burning sun. Presently somebody said, 'Here comes Fatty Burns.' The old chap puts his head and shoulders out of the trench and salaams like a Cairo shopkeeper. We were all struck dumb. Next he climbed out of the trench, which was a bold thing to do, and walked over to our wounded. A dozen rifles were covering him, and I expect he knew it. But Fatty just strolled.

"You could have heard a pin drop, as the saying is. We watched him stroll over to the two men and lift up their heads and give them a drink of water each. He tried to make them comfortable, with us looking on, hardly able to believe our eyes. Then he strolled back quite unconcerned; and we gave him a cheer. That's not all. Just before dusk he came out again, and dragged both men over near a bit of cover, so that we could get them in when dark came. And those are the people that were supposed to be cruel!

"We always had too much bully beef, and when we left the firing line we had to dispose of the surplus and leave the trench in order for those who relieved us. This time we made up our minds to chuck the beef—there were three four-pound tins of it—across to old Fatty Burns. We did, and there was a terrible hullabaloo when it landed. I suppose they thought they were some new-fangled bombs. But an hour or so later some one threw a whole lot of fine dates into the trench, and we reckoned it was Fatty. Some one said they might be poisoned, but we risked that and enjoyed them fine.

"But that's not all. A day or two after we returned to the firing line we got one of our meat-tins back—with additions. I just had time to throw my overcoat down on it when it exploded. The overcoat was never any more good, and it wasn't Fatty Burns's fault that we were sound after the meat-tin came back. He had put in a stick of gelignite and filled up with the remains of an old clock and some spare scraps of iron and things. The clock-wheels fair murdered my overcoat. But what an old sport!

"There was a Maori up on Walker's Ridge who was a very fine swimmer and diver; he could stay under water longer than any man I ever saw. When he was spelling he *would* go in swimming, no matter what the shrapnel was like on the beach. And there was a Turkish sniper up on 'Baby 700' who was after his goat and used to fire at him all the time he was swimming. That made a bit of fun for Te Patara, who used to tantalize the sniper something cruel.

"But these Turks have a lot of time to think, and one day the sniper turned up with a pal and a loader as well. They made it very hot for the Maori gent, who found the bullets arriving two to the second in one long stream. He kept under water and breathed through his ears, or something. Anyhow, he got flustered and made a long dive for the shelter of an iron barge that was stranded on the beach. He got the cover all right and stood up behind the barge in about a foot of water. Abdullah and Co. up in the hills made up their minds to keep him there.

"I should say they got two rifles fixed on each end of the barge and fired them at irregular intervals. And every now and then they would bombard the barge, 'ping, ping,' just to let him know they were watching. It wasn't a particularly warm day; there was a cold sea breeze. Te Patara had no dressing-gown at all, and about two hundred of the boys were down on the beach under cover giving him advice. It was good enough advice, but it was dangerous to take it. He only got away after dark, and then he was the chilliest Maori I ever saw. He seemed to have lost some of his love for swimming, too.

"We reckoned the Turk would not stand up to

the bayonet; and he certainly ran away from it a good many times. Then the First Brigade was sent out to take the trenches at Lonesome Pine, and got the surprise of their lives. A good deal of the fighting was in roofed-in trenches, where it was as dark as Jack Johnson. And there Bismillah stood up and fought with the bayonet. He wasn't a bit particular; if he couldn't use the point he used the butt, clubbing and hacking like a madman. That rough-house in the dark, through 150 yards of underground trenches, was one of the toughest fights of 1915. And the Turk took all the beating the First Brigade could give him. He died fighting, but he would not run.

"Between Anafarta Village and the big salt lake there was a wide valley of agricultural land; the maps do not show how big it is. Before the landing at Suvla Bay all this land was under cultivation, and we used to watch the Turkish farmers at work. They were old boys with big long beards, and we used to imagine them going about saying to one another, ' By the beard of the Prophet,' and things like that. But we decided they were quite harmless, and we let them get in their crops without touching them in any way. A good many of us were thinking of the crops ripening 8,000 miles away south, and us not there to help get them in. So we let these farmers do as they pleased.

"Then came the landing at Suvla; and do you

know these old boys raked up great long Snider rifles from somewhere, that fired an expanding bullet big enough to kill an elephant. One of my mates was hit with one, and it blew the shoulder clean off him. And these old boys fought as bitter as poison. Then the Regular Turkish Army came there, and when the officers found out what these farmers were doing, they kicked up an awful row and took the old guns away from them. We noticed that they went out of use very suddenly, and a prisoner we took told us how it happened. But it shows that the Turks want to fight fair; and that was our experience always.

"This prisoner was a curious fellow. He spoke as good English as I did, and he told me that he used to serve coffee at a big London restaurant. He said he used to go round in a Turkish uniform with a sort of truck, and make special Turkish coffee for those who wanted it. Of course, I did not believe that; where's the sense of it? But he told me a lot of things about the Turks I never knew before, and put them in a new light to me. After all they are only fighting for their own country, and every man ought to do that.

"Whoever planned their defences was a master hand. Every trench is enfiladed from some other one, and the lines of defence fall back, each one endangered to the attacker by that behind it. Some of their trenches were nothing but death-traps to anyone who might choose to occupy them, so skilfully were their machine-guns and snipers posted. I can tell you that we learned a lot about trench digging from our despised brother Bismillah before we had been a month at Gallipoli.

"Yes, the Turk has taught us to respect him for a fair and brave fighter and a dashed sight better man than the fat-faced Germans I've seen driving him against our trenches with their revolvers and the flat of their swords. He is a cunning beggar, is Bismillah; but we bear him no malice for that. It is a pity he was dragged into this scrap by those German beasts. They are the enemy we are all longing to have a cut at. But when poor old Bismillah comes charging in droves against our trenches we hardly like to shoot him down with machine-guns. As one of our chaps said. 'It hardly seems fair to take the money.'"

www.ingramcontent.com/pod-product-compliance
Lightning Source LLC
Chambersburg PA
CBHW060830190426
43197CB00039B/2539